The Plant Rescuer

The Plant Rescuer

The book your houseplants want you to read

Sarah Gerrard-Jones

Photography by Emily Stein
Illustrations by Ruth Greatrex

BLOOMSBURY PUBLISHING
LONDON · OXFORD · NEW YORK · NEW DELHI · SYDNEY

Introduction

I don't believe in the notion that people are 'serial plant killers', nor do I believe people are born with 'green fingers'. Growing plants that thrive is simply a case of taking the time to understand what your houseplant needs to survive and what it's conveying through changes in its appearance.

My aim in writing this book is to give houseplants a voice. Yellow, brown, droopy or crispy leaves can be part of the normal life-cycle of a plant – or a cry for help. But all too often we misread these signs or we don't take the time to understand them. Wouldn't it be great to be able to recognise subtle changes in a plant's health and rectify any problems before the plant reaches the point of no return?

I've been rescuing unheard and misunderstood plants for years and I've poured all I've learnt into this book so that you too can recognise the cries for help and save your plants from the compost heap. Everything I know about houseplants I've learnt through the practical act of caring for them and nurturing them back to health. At times, the actions I take may be seen as unorthodox, but if you don't try, how can you succeed?

An unhappy plant can be a great teacher, but only if you take the time to notice. Throwing a plant away because it no longer looks perfect is an easy option, but in doing so you are just perpetuating the cycle of buying and killing plants; understand the symptoms and you'll break the cycle.

The good news is that the solution to a plant problem is rarely complicated – often the smallest adjustment can make the biggest change. There is myriad advice on how to care for plants, but take everything you read as a starting point for your own experimentation and don't let it become a source of stress. It's important to understand the basic science of how plants grow, but overanalysing every aspect of their care can suck the joy out of what should be a mindful, relaxing and enjoyable experience.

Remember that expert advice is so often a documentation of success, whereas failures are rarely acknowledged – this can undermine confidence. Because occasionally, no matter how hard we try to examine and control the growing conditions, some plants will grow while others will die. Plants are living organisms and can defy the rules – ultimately, we can only do so much.

So liberate yourself from regurgitated advice on the internet and learn from what your plants tell you. Don't jump on the bandwagon, stand on the pavement, wave it goodbye and get back to the job of caring for your plants in your own way. Worry less about doing the 'wrong' thing – failure is the key to future success, and each plant that dies is another lesson in what not to do next time.

I hope this book helps you to choose the right plants for you and your home and gives you the confidence to look after them; if a few are saved from the bin, then my work here is done.

My passion for rescues

The first plants I rescued from the bin at my local DIY store were orchids that had finished flowering – no prizes for guessing why they were binned. Seeing them flower again following some basic care inspired me to look for other plants that could be saved before they were thrown away.

I started with easy ones, like a dumb cane (*Dieffenbachia seguine*) that had been damaged. Other than large tears in the leaves it was healthy, but because people prefer perfect-looking plants it was languishing on the shop shelf. You can't mend ripped leaves, so I left it to grow three new ones and then cut the damaged ones off. It had a bad start in life, but rectifying the problem couldn't have been easier, and to see it now – triple the size – brings me so much happiness (see page 123).

I'd experienced such a sense of fulfilment from saving the orchids and seeing the dumb cane grow under my care, I couldn't wait to find my next patient. I stepped up my search, scouring the local plant shop shelves at least once or twice a week looking for neglected and damaged plants. My heart would skip a beat, not when I saw the most beautiful plant, but when I came across the one with the bent stem or crispy brown leaves – it was that plant that I swiftly marched to the till.

Plants I've rescued

My first attempt at saving a plant that had more than cosmetic damage was a young Swiss cheese plant (*Monstera deliciosa*). It had three leaves, but one of them was black. I was still very much a novice houseplant enthusiast, but I could immediately see what had caused the leaf to turn black: it had been planted directly into a decorative pot that didn't have a drainage hole, the soil was damp and the plant wasn't receiving any natural light. I knew if I took it out of that pot it had a chance of recovering, so it came home with me. After repotting and some minor surgery, it began to unfurl a healthy, bright new leaf and many more have emerged since.

There is much to learn from a change in a leaf's colour or texture. Ignore the changes in your plant and you won't learn anything, and it's likely you will make the same mistakes again and again resulting in many plant failures and a waste of your hard-earned money. Plant care doesn't require a degree in botany or horticulture, it takes nothing more than time, interest and a willingness to learn from what the plant is trying to convey through its appearance and from your mistakes.

I hate to think of people who have failed to keep a plant alive simply giving up and closing the door on the idea of getting another. Killing a plant can teach you exactly what not to do next time. Get straight back on that horse and gallop to the nearest plant shop because next time around things will be different. What's to be gained from labelling yourself a plant killer and refusing to buy another? Building a connection with nature, be it through outdoor or indoor gardening, has so many benefits for our wellbeing that it's worth going through the disappointment of losing a few plants in order to reap the rewards when you understand how to keep them alive.

Plants for life

Modern life isn't conducive to good mental health. There has never been greater pressure to be superhuman. Stress and anxiety are a reaction to feeling pulled in all directions and are exacerbated by not having the time to invest in self care. Slowing down, stripping out the 'noise' of daily life and simply focusing on nurturing a plant can help to give our tired brains a much-needed rest and have a renewing effect on our physical and mental wellbeing.

Growing plants, indoors or outdoors, forces us to slow down and be in the moment. Plants grow slowly, they can't be hurried, they don't inhabit our hectic world, they represent a slower pace of life. Focusing our attention on plants feels like taking a long, deep breath and can help to reset a stressed, anxious, exhausted mind.

I ran terrarium workshops for a few years and the thing I loved most was seeing people who had often come straight from work relax as they focused only on the plants they were putting inside the glass jars. A group of chatty friends would become quiet while they carefully dug small holes in the soil to place the plants into, completely absorbed in the simple task. You could feel the atmosphere in the room change from highly charged to calm within the first ten minutes. Everyone would walk out of the workshop in a different state to the one they arrived in. It was lovely to witness the positive impact plants have on wellbeing and nature's ability to calm an overstimulated mind.

As children we view nature with awe and wonder, but as we grow up our culture provides us with evidence that plants and animals exist purely to support the human race. We have been conditioned to see nature as a commodity to be exploited: a tree has more value chopped down than it has living; an elephant tusk is more valuable than the elephant itself. In our self-imposed role as overseers of nature, we can probably agree that we've failed on a monumental scale and that perhaps it's time to realign ourselves with nature rather than lording over it. At a very basic level we need plants to exist and this fact alone should warrant our appreciation and respect.

The resurgence in popularity of houseplants is a sign that people want to once again be enchanted by nature and make space for it in their lives. Buying a plant, swapping cuttings or sowing seeds – just to experience the magic of watching them grow – has become a priority in many people's lives. By placing yourself within the circle of life, in solidarity with plants, you reinvigorate the connection that society works hard to break. Make room for plants, physically and mentally, show them kindness, engage your senses, learn what they love, and in return they will show their gratitude by enriching your life.

Nurture & Grow

A Plant Buyer's Guide

There are only two things I would regard as being 'wrong' when buying a houseplant: firstly, putting a plant's aesthetic value above its basic needs; and secondly, not investing time in learning how to care for it. When choosing a plant, you shouldn't select one purely because of its visual appeal – your choice should primarily be informed by the conditions you can offer that plant within your home. Buying a plant because it will 'bring life' to a bathroom with no light is wrong, as is buying a cactus to 'make a statement' in a dark alcove of your sitting room.

When you buy a plant you are entering into a contractual agreement to provide what it needs to survive. It may sound a bit harsh, but if you don't agree with the terms of this basic contract, then I suggest buying a new cushion or lamp instead.

Outside of those two misdemeanours, there is a world of beautiful, fascinating and characterful plants to choose from that will bring life and colour to your home, make statements and bring you happiness. To help you decide which plant or plants to buy, I've compiled a list of things to think about before making a purchase.

The Myth of the Perfect Plant

We live in a throwaway society in which it is easier and quicker to replace rather than repair. We've moved so far away from the 'make do and mend' mentality of previous generations that we have a tendency to chuck anything away, from faulty appliances and out-of-style clothing to vegetables and plants that are deemed imperfect. A culture obsessed with perfection leads to millions of healthy plants being discarded. They are discarded by the grower, the wholesaler, the shop owner and by us in our own homes – nature is being binned because it doesn't meet our impossibly high standards and ideals.

Often, when I'm out on a walk, I will stamp on or rip from the ground a plant that has a brown leaf. I require all plants to look perfect at all times, and if they don't, it's goodbye plant. My eyes should not have to bear witness to a brown leaf – how dare it exist! As ridiculous as this sounds, this is what we are doing when we demand a refund from an online plant seller if our plant arrives with a ripped leaf, or when we ignore the plant that leans to the side and is languishing on the bottom shelf at the garden centre. Plants in nature are not 'perfect', so why do we require them to be pristine before we buy them?

Increasingly, houseplants are being viewed as short-lived disposable items, much like a wilted bunch of flowers, and one of the regular victims of our throwaway culture is the orchid. It's common practice at supermarkets, petrol stations, DIY shops and even garden centres to throw out orchids once they've finished flowering. It was seeing this happen at my local DIY shop that started my obsession with rescuing plants. The sight of healthy plants, midway through their life-cycle, being thrown away like broken toys saddened me so deeply, that a need to rescue as many plants as possible was born.

It's not just shopkeepers who bin orchids. I've heard of houseplant owners discarding their orchids after they've flowered, too. And perhaps they are justified: you bought an orchid (or were gifted it), and you expected it to flower for the rest of its life, but after a mere three months, the flowers wilted and fell off, leaving just a stalk and some green leaves. This is not what you should have to see – you expected flowers, not just leaves! Frankly, I'm outraged that it has the gall to take up space in your house looking like *that* for the next nine months while it builds up energy to flower again. How dare it! You were right to throw it away and I'm sorry that the orchid duped you into thinking that it would always look perfect. Perhaps it should come with a warning label: 'will be offensive to the eye after flowering'.

I'm sure most people don't really think this way or really want to dispose of their plants, but nurture and repair require time, which is difficult to find in our hectic schedules. And this lack of time and care is why throwing a plant away after it flowers and buying another one in bloom has sadly become so common. If you care for an orchid it will flower again and again. If you learn to appreciate the period in between flowering as part of the plant's life-cycle, you will have a houseplant you love for years to come.

The joy of an orchid for me, as with every other plant, is watching it grow. Seeing a flower spike emerge, then buds appearing which burst open into a cascade of impossibly beautiful flowers, is awe-inspiring. Just imagining this happening blows my mind, but actually seeing it happen before my eyes is incredible! Why would you want to miss out on the best part? Sadly, many hundreds of thousands if not millions of orchids lose their lives after they stop flowering – and the environmental impact of growing more cannot be ignored.

Plant production is a multi-billion-pound industry and with it comes all the environmental costs associated with mass production: energy and water consumption, peat consumption, chemical use, emissions from air and freight travel, not to mention the amount of non-biodegradable plastic used. Those of us who buy houseplants like to think of our hobby as being 'green', but houseplant production has a large environmental footprint, made even greater by our unwillingness to accept anything but absolute perfection. Plants are green, but plant production is not.

It's troubling to think about the harm that growing plants on a massive scale has on the environment, which is possibly why many of us never consider it. If you were aware of the fossil fuel consumption needed to grow a plant and make a plastic pot (which will still be on this planet centuries from now), or the neonicotinoid pesticides used to keep insects at bay (which damage bees' ability to reproduce), perhaps you might be less relaxed about the plant and its pot being discarded because of an 'imperfection'.

Our instinct when looking for plants is to choose the most pristine looking one on the shelf because we think it must be healthier, more resilient and therefore less likely to die than its slightly less polished counterpart. It's similar to the way we might avoid picking up a misshapen vegetable because our perception is that it won't taste as nice as a straight one, though in reality we know they will most likely taste the same. A plant with a ripped leaf or a slightly bent stem is no less healthy than one without a ripped leaf and a straighter stem. It could be that the 'perfect' one hasn't been knocked over, or squashed against the side of a lorry or been sat in a draught. Take a closer look at the less-than-perfect one, check it doesn't have pests and consider taking this one home instead. You can change the outcome for this plant, you can make a difference and vote with your purchasing power – by saving it from being thrown away you are standing against the binning of healthy plants.

I usually avoid buying the perfect-looking plant because I know someone else will, but who will buy the one with the torn or brown leaf? A torn leaf can be cut off, a brown leaf might be a sign that it's in need of a drink. Are you really going to let that sad plant, sitting on the bottom shelf in the dark, get thrown away because it simply needs some light?

 Clues to why the plant looks unhappy can be very obvious when you look at where it's been placed in the shop. Is it getting enough light? Is the potting mix very dry or very wet? These are easy things for you to rectify: you can put it in a bright spot to let the soil dry out, or you can give it a drink. None of these things are difficult and recovery can be swift, sometimes within a week.

The sense of achievement from seeing a neglected plant flourish in your care, knowing it would otherwise have been thrown away, is addictive. Why else do you think I can barely move for rescued plants in my house? If you don't choose the one with the broken stem or ripped leaf, it may never get the chance to grow, and the energy and water used to make the pot and grow the plant will have been wasted. Where's the harm in trying? There is so much to be gained from nurturing a sad plant back to health, lessons that no amount of scrolling on the internet can teach you.

'Imperfect' plants

Purchasing Plants

In an ideal world, we'd all do masses of research into plant species before ever stepping into a plant shop. Before buying any plant, we'd be fully clued up, knowing where the plant originates from and where it would be best suited to living in our home. In reality, things aren't quite so organised. Chances are, you'll make a spontaneous visit to a plant shop and buy three plants (none of which are suitable for your dark basement flat) because you just couldn't resist. Let's be honest, when we see a beautiful plant that makes our heart palpitate, we buy it without considering the details – then we bring it home and put it where we think it looks best.

Buying a plant because 'we just had to have it' is part of the joy of owning houseplants, but your love affair could quickly sour if you can't or don't provide the right conditions for that species. The reason we want to grow plants is because they bring us pleasure (we don't buy them to bring us disappointment), but so often sadness is the predominant feeling we are left with after watching the plant's health decline. Remember, plant murdering isn't a condition we're afflicted with; we can all be happy plant owners with happy plants if we choose the plant that's right for our home.

So it's best to think ahead, understand the conditions your home can provide and choose a plant that suits you (see page 100). That initial research is the first step to a long-lasting, happy and healthy relationship which need not end in dead plants and tears.

Once you've established the species of plant that will enjoy the conditions you can provide, it's time to shop.

Buying in store

Sadly, you are not allowed to test drive plants before purchase, but you are allowed to give your plant the once over before agreeing to hand over your hard-earned cash. Giving the plant a health check before buying it is imperative. You wouldn't buy a car without giving it a thorough examination and you shouldn't buy a plant without doing so either. Prevention is always better than cure, so make sure every effort is made to inspect the plant of your dreams before taking it to the till.

My advice is to buy a small magnifying glass to take with you on plant shopping excursions; plant pests are minuscule and can be extremely difficult to spot, so why take any chances? Look for tiny white, brown or yellow specks that live on, under or in between leaves or stems (see page 216 for identification). If you see evidence of pest excretions or the pests themselves, I would advise against buying that plant unless you are prepared to remedy the problem.

I would also suggest keeping new houseplants away from any other plants in your home for the first week – this is to ensure that your plant isn't showing signs of a pest infestation. Pests can hop to other plants and the last thing you want is to introduce an infestation that can have devastating results. Once you deem it safe and totally free of pests, it can be integrated among the others.

Online shopping

Buying online has become one of the most popular ways to shop for plants. It can be a great way to grow your collection, but it's worth remembering that the plant will have to be shipped, potentially from across the country, before it reaches you. It would be miraculous if every plant arrived in a perfect state, because they go through a lot: generally, they are wrapped up, pushed into a dark box, thrown around in vans and warehouses, and land on your doorstep several turbulent days later. I wonder how you might look and feel after this experience – perhaps a little bruised, or worse, suffering a broken limb or two. If you order a plant online, you have to accept that it might get damaged on the way. Coming to terms with this realisation will avoid disappointment, so instead of huffing about a ripped leaf, think about what the plant has had to endure to arrive in your home and show it some love. Give it the best spot in the house and leave it to acclimatise (see page 33).

As online sales of plants grow, so do the mountains of plants that get discarded, often before they even make it into the box. Online sellers are reluctant to send a plant if it has even the slightest imperfection for fear the buyer will complain or demand a refund. The more complaints a retailer gets, the more inclined they are to throw away healthy plants just because they don't look perfect. Most of us now agree that throwing away vegetables because they're wonky shouldn't be an acceptable practice, and yet there are houseplants being discarded on a massive scale for the same reason.

Unless the plant you ordered arrives in woefully poor condition or infested with pests, it's better to assist it than complain. You can perform minor surgery on ripped leaves with the snip of scissors (though you don't have to cut off leaves if they don't bother you), and if a stem has been broken, you can propagate it (see page 228), then you'll have two plants for the price of one.

I'd like to see online retailers offering the 'less-than-perfect' plants at a discounted price, rather than needlessly throwing them away. How about a section for characterful plants, with bent stems or a few missing leaves? It's about time we gave up these ideas of what a perfect plant should look like and embrace their uniqueness. A true plant lover loves all plants regardless of their looks; a plant perfectionist is not a plant lover. Which team will you choose? Perfectionist or Lover? Make the right choice and join me on team Plant Lover.

Before buying online, consider the following:
— Read customer reviews. Trust in the store's service before you part with your money.
— Read the small print. It's unlikely you'll be sent the exact plant in the photo and reading the details will give you a better idea of what to expect, for example, it might not be the same size, shape or even colour. It's also good to check on the store's environmental policy.
— Check the returns policy. If you're not happy with what arrives, it's good to know your rights.
— Opt for the quickest delivery method. This limits any potential damage and is particularly relevant in winter, as the longer the plant is in a box in cold weather, the more likely it is to suffer.

Secondhand purchases

Shopping for a new plant is undeniably exciting, but there are other ways to acquire plants to expand your collection. Trading cuttings with friends or buying plants secondhand is often my preference.

Well-known online sites such as eBay, Facebook Marketplace and Gumtree (there may also be other sites in your area) can be great places to find houseplants. The most unusual and interesting plants in my collection are secondhand finds, because they automatically come with a history (in some cases they are decades old), and they are always full of character. I love imagining what these plants must have seen during their lives, how many different places they may have lived and why they are being passed on to someone else. There is an emotional connection in buying a plant from someone's home, where it may have been loved and nurtured for many years, which feels entirely different to picking up a new plant in a shop. On many occasions I have arrived to collect a plant and the owner will say, 'I just want it to go to a good home' – it's as though they are giving away a pet. In response, I whip out my phone and show them my collection – they are delighted that it will be well cared for.

Shopping secondhand is also a great way to find plants that may need rescuing. Sometimes I'm compelled to buy a plant because it looks in a bad way and I know I could give it a better life, or because it's so weird-looking that I can't imagine anyone else wanting it.

If you're planning on buying secondhand, here are a few tips:
— Set your search area. There is no point getting excited about a huge cactus that's 300 miles away. Decide how far you're willing to travel to collect a plant before you start shopping online.
— Look closely at all the photos. Can you spot any potential issues with the plant? This needn't be a deal breaker, but it's best to be aware of any work that needs to be done, such as immediate repotting.
— Ask questions. Don't be afraid to ask what condition the plant is in, if the pot that is photographed is included and whether the plant comes from a non-smoking household. (I know of people who have bought plants that smelled of stale smoke.)
— Don't be afraid to barter. If you don't ask, you don't get.
— Check the plant for signs of pests. When you pick up, and before agreeing to the sale, always check for pests.

Plant Poaching

The desire to fill our homes with plants stems from a need to be connected to nature, but ironically it is fuelling the rampant destruction of delicate habitats and biodiversity by poachers. The illegal trafficking of plants has mostly remained an underground topic, but the media is starting to shine a light on the growing problem. The huge surge in demand

for houseplants has led to an alarming increase in the number of plants being ripped from their natural environment by illegal traders. It's a complex issue, but where there is a market there will always be people willing to exploit the wild, which is why reporting of this global crisis needs to be stepped up and why we all need to be aware of what we are buying and who we are buying it from. We need to make it our responsibility to ensure we buy plants from reputable sources. Shockingly many illegally poached, protected plant species can be found easily on well-known online auction sites.

So how do you know if the plant you are interested in buying has been raised in a nursery or been stolen from the wild? Look closely at the photos: the plants we buy from nurseries don't usually have imperfections in the same way as plants in the wild. Commercially grown plants are raised in ideal conditions, whereas those in nature have suffered all weathers and this will show in their appearance. The plants offered for sale may even be photographed in their natural habitat or shown with soil on their roots, ripped from the ground. If you are in any doubt about the plant's origins, ask the seller questions. If you aren't convinced by the answers or if they avoid answering questions, trust your instinct and don't buy it. You should also make the site aware of your suspicions so they can remove access to sellers suspected of plant poaching.

The trade in rare plants, which command astronomical prices, is also a cause for concern. Be aware that even if you're buying from a reputable source, your purchase has a knock on effect, as poachers target popular, high value plants and pull them from their natural habitats. I understand the desire to fill our homes with beautiful plants, but it shouldn't cost the earth. It is our planet that is ultimately paying the price.

Acclimatising Plants

Within the first week or month of bringing home a new plant, you might notice that it doesn't look as great as it did when you bought it. Don't panic. Your plant is adjusting to the new conditions in your home, making vital adaptations to survive. It might lose a few leaves or even some of the vigour that attracted you to it in the first place. Its original home likely felt

like a luxury retreat, and since leaving its happy place, your plant has endured fluctuating temperatures, unreliable light levels and sporadic watering. It is no longer sunning itself on a beach, sipping coconut water through a straw, it's working hard to adapt to a new way of life. Leaves that have turned brown/yellow/lighter/darker or even fallen off are all normal occurrences when a plant has experienced dramatic changes in its environmental conditions. Don't be tempted to move it or repot it, the last thing it needs right now is more change. Resist the urge to panic and fuss.

What your plant needs is to be reminded of that wonderful holiday, where it basked in hours of diffused sun, helping itself to the all-inclusive buffet with drinks on tap. Your aim should be to reduce the amount of stress on your plant by creating the ultimate package-holiday in your own home. Think like a travel agent and know your client: desert cacti would not enjoy a holiday anywhere dark, and calatheas would be horrified to be sent somewhere with 12 hours of direct blazing sun. To make your life, and your plant's life, easier I've compiled a list of popular houseplants and where they are best suited to living in your home (see page 100).

Understanding Plants

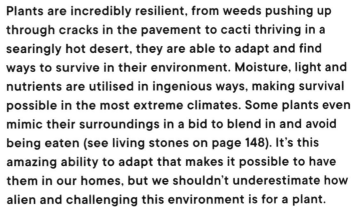

Plants are incredibly resilient, from weeds pushing up through cracks in the pavement to cacti thriving in a searingly hot desert, they are able to adapt and find ways to survive in their environment. Moisture, light and nutrients are utilised in ingenious ways, making survival possible in the most extreme climates. Some plants even mimic their surroundings in a bid to blend in and avoid being eaten (see living stones on page 148). It's this amazing ability to adapt that makes it possible to have them in our homes, but we shouldn't underestimate how alien and challenging this environment is for a plant.

Most of our homes are at least 50% darker than the outside world, and unless we remove the roof, there is no natural source of water. Given that they rely upon us to provide them with everything they need to survive, it is little wonder that the plants we bring into our homes sometimes struggle to do well.

Plants must have light, water, warmth and nutrients to grow, without these basics they will die. Put a hamster in a cage and you've taken away its ability to survive without our intervention; it's a similar story for a plant in a pot, but unlike the hamster, the houseplant can make adjustments to increase its chances of survival within these artificial surroundings. With their roots encased in a pot, less than ideal light, much drier air and chemically cleansed water, plants manage to survive by adapting to their environment. Forgive them if they shed a few leaves or elongate a stem to reach for light; be amazed rather than disappointed at their resilience in the face of adversity.

Photosynthesis

Survival of all plants, whether in the wild or in our homes, relies on them being able to photosynthesise. The inner workings of a plant are like the cogs of a well-oiled machine. When the plant is in the ideal environmental conditions, the cogs turn smoothly, producing the right amount of food for the plant to be in good health. Changing just one aspect of the environment – such as moving the plant from bright light to low light – throws a spanner in the works, and food production slows until it eventually grinds to a halt, leaving a once perfectly healthy plant starving to death. Plants will try their best to adapt in order to survive, but some just can't adapt quickly enough, or are less capable than others, and despite their best efforts, sadly won't make it.

When faced with a challenging environment, certain plants are able to adapt readily, altering the concentration of chloroplasts to respond to lower or brighter light conditions. Plants recommended for low light are simply those that are better able to do this than others – given the choice, most would rather not have to adapt, but if it's a matter of survival they will. I haven't come across many plants that leap out of your arms, barge through the front door and race across the room to claim the shadiest spot, but I've met plenty that sigh, shrug their shoulders, shuffle over there and get on with the task of quietly making do with less.

Three essential components plants need in order to survive are light, carbon dioxide and water – yes, this may sound basic, but you'd be surprised by how many people ask me: which plants can live in a bathroom with no light? Having basic knowledge of your plant's survival needs is paramount and gives you a better chance of keeping your houseplant alive and thriving. (By the way, the answer to the bathroom question is: no plant can survive long-term in any room without light.)

Without the right intensity of light, the first stage of photosynthesis can't take place. Carbon dioxide is present in the air and (hopefully) there is water in the soil, but it is light that triggers the process of converting these elements into oxygen and glucose, which is the source of energy for plant growth. Remove light or provide too little light for your plant and this process will not happen.

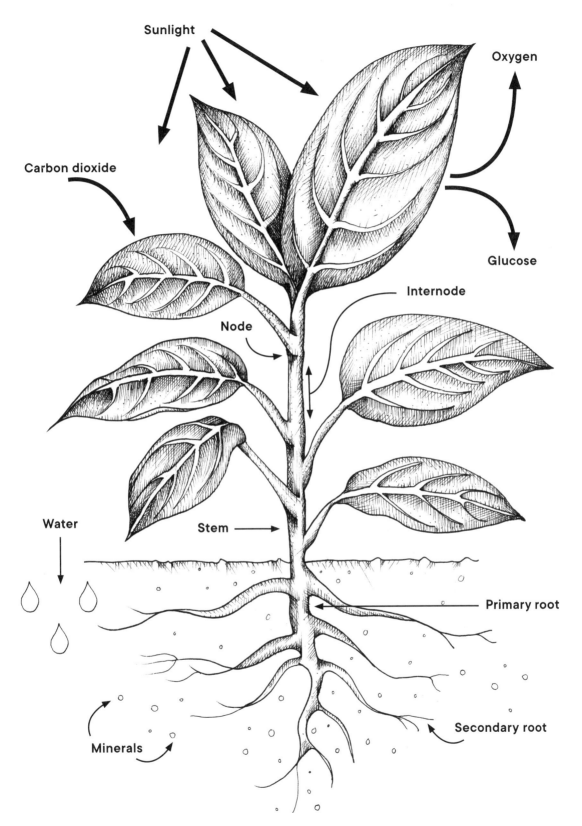

Sunlight

Oxygen

Carbon dioxide

Glucose

Internode

Node

Stem

Water

Primary root

Minerals

Secondary root

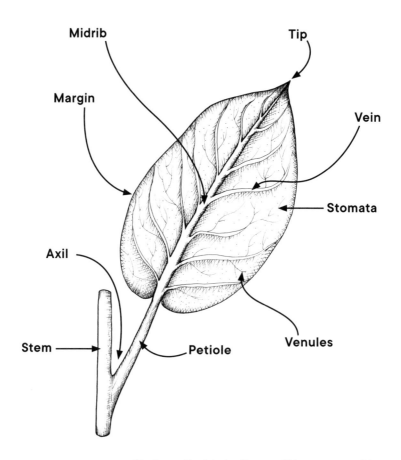

Midrib

Tip

Margin

Vein

Stomata

Axil

Stem

Petiole

Venules

Carbon dioxide isn't something we need to concern ourselves with as it's already present in the air, but it's nevertheless a vital element in the process. Without carbon dioxide diffusing into the plant via stomata on the leaves, combining with water drawn up from the roots, the light that hits the chlorophyll in the leaves won't trigger photosynthesis. All elements must be present for the process to take effect.

Plant roots absorb water, along with nutrients and minerals present in the soil, and these are transported by the xylem to the stem and then the leaves, where the magic happens. The pigment in the chloroplast – chlorophyll – absorbs light from the sun and uses this energy to convert carbon dioxide and water into glucose and oxygen. The plant is interested in the glucose for food but expels oxygen as a waste product. Surprisingly, less than 5% of water is used by the plant for the actual process of photosynthesis. Transpiration, an unavoidable consequence of photosynthesis, uses up a large percentage of the water. Transpiration is the movement of water through a plant and its evaporation through areas such as the leaves, stems and flowers. Transpiration acts like an air-conditioning system, cooling the leaves as it evaporates from the plant. The rate of transpiration increases and decreases with changes in environmental conditions. Raised temperature and light increase the rate of transpiration and this is one of the main reasons that plants need more water in summer compared with in winter.

The rate that plants are able to photosynthesise depends on the levels of light, temperature and water, as well as the concentration of carbon dioxide in the air and the amount of chlorophyll the plant has. Generally, the deeper the shade of green of the leaf, the greater the mass of chlorophyll, and the greater its light-absorbing ability. Broadly speaking, the greater the presence of chlorophyll, the better chance the plant has of adapting to lower-than-ideal light conditions. Pale-coloured or variegated leaves have less chlorophyll than green leaves and need more light to photosynthesise, which makes them susceptible to failure in poor light. Different plants have different amounts of chlorophyll, and this is not only governed by their natural environment, but can also vary due to certain factors such as disease and a lack of nutrients – these can damage the chloroplasts and reduce their ability to make chlorophyll.

We all know that feeling of excitement when we bring a beautiful, exotic, glossy-leaved plant home and can't wait to nurture it and watch it grow, but sadly, despite our best intentions, we also know that feeling when it starts looking sad, brown and droopy. Getting a plant to survive in our home, let alone thrive, can only be achieved by understanding the conditions in which it grows in the wild.

Let's imagine I'm used to living in a hot country, where the air is dry and most of the year it's sunny. You invite me to come and visit your country and stay in your house that is cold, draughty, humid and dark. In all honesty, I might be a little bit unhappy while visiting you because it's very different to what I'm used to, I haven't adapted to this climate and I really want to be somewhere warm and dry. This scenario plays out when you put a desert cactus in a dark bathroom: it will not be happy because these conditions are unlike those it is designed and adapted to live in.

Match the light that your plant receives in its natural environment with what is available in your home and you will stand a good chance of your plant surviving – get the temperature, amount of water and potting mix right, and these things combined will create good conditions for your plant to happily photosynthesise.

Taking the time to understand how plants live is time well spent, and the reward for your willingness to learn will be your plant not dying. I will forgive you for being asleep in your biology lesson, but I will not, after reading this book, forgive you for putting a plant in a bathroom with no window! There are solutions for low light areas of your home and there are plants that will tolerate lower light better than others (see page 106), but understanding how light affects your plant's ability to grow may make you reconsider leaving it in the dark.

Crassulacean acid metabolism

Crassulacean acid metabolism (CAM) is an ingenious plant adaptation. The name comes from the *Crassula* genus, which led to the discovery of CAM. It is performed primarily by succulents and allows them to minimise water loss in extreme temperatures. Most plants open their stomata during the day, but in extremely hot, arid environments, when water is lost quickly through transpiration, plants practising CAM can close their stomata to conserve it. Closed stomata can't absorb carbon dioxide (CO_2), which is essential for photosynthesis, so they open them in the cool of the night to absorb CO_2 and store it. This allows the plant to conserve water and photosynthesise without opening their stomata during the day.

Light

All plants need light to survive: light is essential in order for plants to create food. Humans can survive for a period of time without food, but we will eventually die of starvation, and it is the same for plants. However, unlike humans, plants are able to make their own food (see Photosynthesis on page 38), but houseplants are reliant on you to meet their basic needs in order to do this effectively.

Too much water is often thought to be the number one killer of houseplants, but water alone isn't the culprit, water has an accomplice called light, and it's when these two get together in unequal amounts that murder is committed. Get the lighting right and your plant stands a much better chance

of survival. There is so much confusion surrounding how much light plants need and this uncertainty is a major cause of unhealthy plants and plant deaths. Just because we think a room looks bright, it doesn't necessarily mean that it is providing your plant with lots of bright light.

Humans and plants perceive light differently: lumens, lux and foot candles are three units that measure how we perceive light, but they do not accurately describe the quality of light that's of use to a plant for photosynthesis. Photosynthetic active radiation (PAR) is the portion of light used by plants for photosynthesis. A room lit by a domestic lightbulb appears bright to our eyes, but it may as well be total darkness for a plant (unless the plant is receiving PAR from a window or a specialist grow light).

Plants don't see light as we see it, they sense it in light-sensitive proteins called photoreceptors. We see the full spectrum of visible light, but are most sensitive to yellowish-green wavelengths. Plants sense a slightly wider spectrum of light (including some ultraviolet and infrared wavelengths), but are mostly interested in red and blue wavelengths. The information the photoreceptors receive when they sense certain wavelengths triggers numerous reactions within the plant, the most important being photosynthesis. It is our job to ensure that they receive enough light for this to happen.

This may sound complex, but all I'm really saying is that you need to position your plants close enough to a window so that they can sense the light. Intensity of light increases the closer we get to any window, regardless of which direction it faces – we can see this and the plant can sense it. But if you'd prefer to take the guesswork out of where to position your plants, you can download a light meter app to any smartphone which will tell you if the light intensity is enough to drive photosynthesis.

For decades, humans have enjoyed decorating their interiors with plants, but plants need to be treated as nature, not furniture, if they are to thrive. We live in semi-shade in our homes, with even the brightest rooms being considerably darker than the outdoors. Position a plant just a few feet back from a window and you're reducing the amount of light by at least 50%, if not more. The further away a plant is from a source of light (window or grow light), the less likely it is to remain healthy and the more likely it is to develop an ailment or be attacked by pests. A plant that gets the right amount of light (and water) will grow; one that is in low light can struggle to survive.

At a concert it's exciting to be near the stage, that's why those spaces fill up first – it's a more immersive experience than being further back. For your plant, the room is a concert venue and the stage is the window. The plant wants to be close to the stage because that's where the excitement is. When pigments inside the plant are excited by light, chemical processes are kickstarted which lead to photosynthesis. If, like me, you are vertically challenged, you might spend most concerts unable to see the stage, which is similar to the view a plant sitting at the back of your room has – and I know how disappointing that is. You have the ability to make sure your plant gets the best view! Don't put it in the cheap seats at the back, give it the VIP treatment by placing it close to the window. A ticket upgrade costs nothing more than picking up your plant and walking it to the front row.

Common terms

Bright light
This encompasses two types of light: direct and indirect. Bright direct light means there is nothing (other than the clear glass in the window frame) obstructing the light reaching your plant. The sun's rays are directly hitting the plant through the window. Meanwhile, bright indirect light means that the sun's rays aren't directly hitting the plant. Indirect can also mean partially filtered light – this is light that is passing through something before it reaches your plant, for example leaves on a tree outside or a semi-opaque window covering. Indirect light can still be considered bright, but is not as intense and is unlikely to burn a plant's leaves. The brightest light is most likely to be found coming through a south-facing window.

Moderate light
A plant in moderate light may get a few hours of bright direct light, but for the majority of the day it would receive indirect light, which is less intense. Moderate light indoors can be described as partial shade and it may also be determined by the plant's distance from the window or by an object, building or other obstruction diffusing or blocking the light before it reaches the plant.

Low light

This type of light can be found in areas of your home that are permanently shaded due to the direction the window faces, or due to light being obscured by an external or internal object (such as a building or semi-closed blind). This term also relates to the distance of the plant from a window – the further away the plant, the lower the light intensity. Direct sunlight never makes an appearance in an area of low light.

Window direction

This is a basic guide to the light received by standard-size windows facing in different directions based on summer in the Northern Hemisphere. If you don't know which direction your windows face, use a compass or download a compass app to your phone. Do remember that 'close to a window' doesn't mean below it, where the plant doesn't reach the glass, or beside it on the same wall, which is deep shade. For more information on which plant to place where, see page 100.

South-facing window

Plants that require bright light or bright indirect light will enjoy being within 30–60cm (1–2ft) of a south-facing window. The only plants that will tolerate being in direct light all day on a windowsill are desert cacti and certain succulents. It's best not to place foliage plants on a windowsill that receives direct light for most of the day, as they might get burnt.

East- or west-facing window

Bright to moderate light can be found beside or no further than 60–90cm (2–3ft) back, from an east- or west-facing window where direct light will reach the plant for only part of the day. The majority of foliage plants will be happy here, apart from those that prefer a shadier area.

North-facing window

Low light can be found by a north-facing window, where no direct sunlight reaches the window. A plant needs to be close to a north-facing window (within 30cm/1ft) to stand the best chance of survival.

While this is a useful guide to understanding light intensity, it doesn't take into account the many variables of your particular windows or where you live. A south-facing window usually

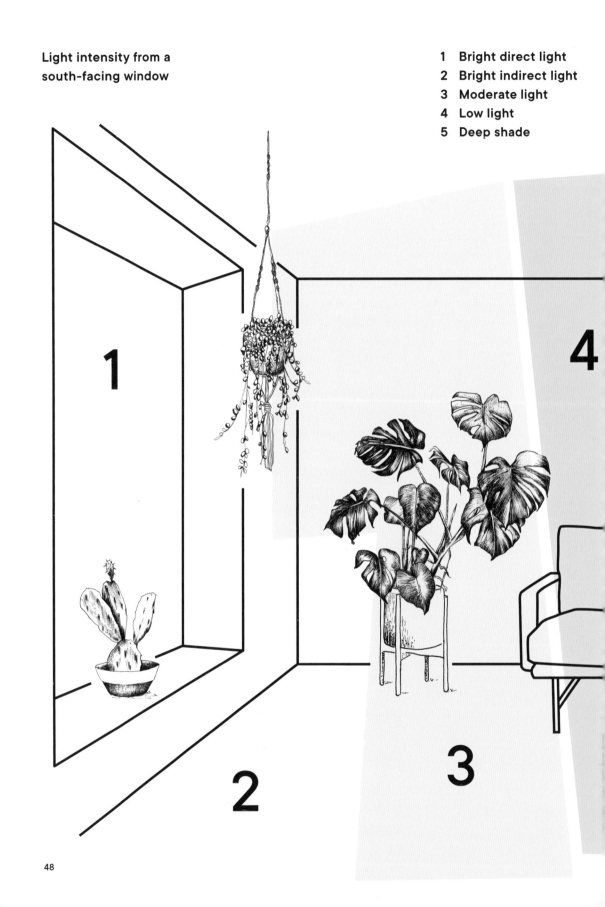

Light intensity from a
south-facing window

1 Bright direct light
2 Bright indirect light
3 Moderate light
4 Low light
5 Deep shade

1

4

2

3

5

provides the brightest light, but only if it isn't shaded by anything outside like a large tree or building. The direct light inside can be partially shielded or diffused by slatted blinds or frosted glass – this could make a south-facing window an option for some foliage plants as the light is less intense. Your geographical location, the size of your window, how deeply it is recessed and the colour of your walls (darker colours absorb light, while white reflects it) all have an impact on light intensity. Where best to place your plant is something only you can work out. Everyone's home has different levels of light in different areas and it's these variables that ensure rules about where to position plants are impossible to make or follow.

Cleaning

While we're on the subject of what can affect the amount of light coming through your window, I'd like to mention cleaning. It's not something I'm known to be a fan of, but when it comes to houseplants, I will do absolutely anything to keep them happy, and that includes a bit of light housework. Grubby windows can reduce the amount of light your plants receive, so give them a wash inside and out.

While you're in cleaning mode, think about dust, too. Dust accumulates on all surfaces in our home and that includes our plants. A layer of dust, no matter how thin, will reduce the amount of light that hits the leaves and can inhibit the plant's ability to photosynthesise (it's also good to check that the dust isn't a sign of a spider mite infestation, see page 216). Get into the habit of wiping leaves at least once a month using a damp cloth. Alternatively, move the plants into the shower and give them a spray; let them drip dry and then wipe their leaves dry before moving them back. Don't forget to dust your cacti and succulents – I find a small paint brush works best. I've heard of people using milk or mayonnaise to clean leaves – I would never do this, partly because I'm vegan, but I also wouldn't risk clogging up the stomata with products like this. Water and a cloth works perfectly well. There is no need for your plant to have shiny leaves, only for it to be free from dust so it can absorb the maximum amount of light possible.

Grow lights

Don't despair if the light in your house, flat, studio or office isn't ideal for growing plants, there are a few easy ways to rectify this problem. Minor changes can help, such as painting a coloured wall white and strategically placing mirrors to reflect and bounce light around the room, but to make a real difference you might consider investing in a grow light or two. Not only can they provide the optimum amount of light to aid photosynthesis, but they can also be placed in dark areas and make it possible to have plants anywhere in your home – a dream come true! This opens the opportunity to cram every nook and cranny with plants; window or no window, plants are possible. It's literally a lightbulb moment!

In simple terms, grow lights can be used to increase the intensity of light in your home, which is helpful for those who live in dark houses, with few or small windows, or windows that face the wrong direction. They can also be helpful in counteracting the drop in light levels during autumn and winter. Domestic lightbulbs provide light for us to be able to see and can make the room look bright, but alone they don't provide plants with enough photosynthetic light to survive long-term.

Think of grow lights and you might imagine large, industrial contraptions, suspended from the ceiling like an upside-down snooker table. Thankfully, this is no longer the only option and grow lights needn't make your home look like a marijuana factory. There are a huge number on the market to choose from, including many options designed to be aesthetically pleasing. They don't have to be a big financial investment either – there are many affordable options available, from LED strips that can be stuck beneath a shelf to bulbs that screw into your existing light fittings.

In fact, there is a baffling number of grow lights to choose from and I'm going to admit that specialist knowledge would be required to go deep into this topic (there are entire books just on grow lights). To get you started, here is a simplistic guide to grow lights starting with the terms you might come across.

Wattage The higher the wattage the brighter the light.

Lumens A measure of the amount of light visible to humans. More lumens means brighter light.

Kelvin Colour temperature/the colour of light produced by the bulb. Lights that give off a 'warm' glow are somewhere from 2700-3500k – and look nice in our homes. The

higher numbers (around 4000–4500k) are often used in offices, while lights around 5000–6500k are referred to as 'full spectrum' and best match the colour of natural daylight. As kelvins get higher, they look more blue. Blue light looks clean but cold. Foliage growth is generally best around 5000–6500k.

PAR Photosynthetic active radiation is the portion of light spectrum used in photosynthesis, which is from 400–700 nanometres.

The two main options when it comes to bulb colour are full spectrum grow lights, which replicate the light of the sun by emitting all the colours of the spectrum, and red/blue grow lights – blue light generally stimulates growth, while red light is important for growth and flowering. Different plants require different ratios of red and blue, so a combination might work better for some than others. If you don't like the disco-pink glow emitted by red/blue grow lights, opt for full spectrum that give off a white light. Both will provide your plants with light suitable for growth, so really your choice might come down to cost and colour preference.

LED and fluorescent bulbs both produce the full spectrum light that plants need to grow. LEDs use only a fraction of the electricity used by normal incandescent bulbs and are cheaper to run than fluorescent bulbs.

How far to place your plant from the grow light depends on the type of plant and how intense the light is. The higher the wattage and lumens, the stronger and more intense it will be. It may say in the instructions how far the plant should be placed from the light, but if it doesn't, experiment. If your plant isn't growing or is reaching toward the light, then the light may need to be moved closer. A plant placed too close will get burnt tips (not from heat, from light). It may need to be as close as 5cm (2in) or as far as 60cm (2ft).

How many hours you keep the light on is also something that depends on the plant and the type of light. As a rough guide, expect foliage plants to need around 12 hours of light, while cacti and succulents will need about 14 hours. All plants benefit from a period of rest, so I would advise against keeping them on 24 hours a day.

Phototropism and nastic responses

Plants can move their leaves in response to stimuli such as light, reaching towards it for more – this is known as phototropism, a directional growth response to light. Plants can also respond to non-directional factors, such as darkness, which is known as a nastic response.

If you were to stay up all night and stare at your prayer plant (see page 111), you might witness it moving its leaves from a horizontal position to an almost vertical one as the sun goes down, then back down again in the morning as the sun comes up. Is the plant sleeping? No, but its biology functions on a similar circadian rhythm to ours, which is why Darwin documented this phenomenon as the 'sleep movements of leaves'. More recent theories about why plants may close their leaves at night include to stop water falling on them and to protect them from fungi and bacteria that take up residence in warm, moist environments.

The sensitive plant (*Mimosa pudica*) performs another type of nastic movement, closing up when touched. This is thought to be a defence against being eaten by animals, and this type of movement is described as thigmonastic movement. Brush past the leaves of the plant and the cells that make up the pulvinus (at the base of the petiole), enlarge and shrink due to water pressure that causes the leaves to be pulled upwards or downwards.

There is ongoing research into what impact touch may have on plants. One study (conducted by a professor of plant science, Jim Whelan) found that even the lightest touch or gentle pat by a human hand could reduce a plant's growth rate by as much as 30%, while an earlier study (by biologist Floriane L'Haridon) suggests that touch could be beneficial in stimulating the plant's immune system. Regardless of which is true, the findings may cause us to think differently about our interactions with the plants around us.

Putting your plants outside

During the warmer months of the year, many houseplants will appreciate a stint outdoors. The level of light, even in the shade, will be much higher than inside, the rain will wash and water them, and any pests will be reduced. If you decide to put them outside, there are a few things you need to do:

— Slowly introduce them to the outside world. Put them in a semi-shaded spot that's sheltered from the wind for a few

hours a day, then bring them back inside. Extend the time you leave them out until they are outside full-time, but never where they could be burnt by the sun or damaged by the wind.
— Don't put them out on the hottest day of the year and forget about them – they could burn, wilt or even die.
— Check on them daily to see if they need water and make sure pests aren't taking an interest.
— Check the weather forecast every day and bring them back indoors if there is a chance of extreme wind, rain or very high temperatures.
— Always keep a very close eye on how your plant is responding to being outside and bring it back inside if it shows any signs of being unhappy, such as wilting, leaf drop or scorching.
— Bring them back inside well before the temperature drops. Give them a once over to check for hitch-hikers such as worms, earwigs, snails and beetles, which we love outside, but not in the house.

Watering

'How often should I water my plant?' It's a common question, but without knowing everything about the environment the plant is being kept in, it's impossible to offer a definitive answer. There are no rules that can be followed when it comes to watering because there are so many variables to consider: the type of plant, the amount of light, the temperature, the type of pot, the size of pot and the conditions of the room all play a part. A hanging plant will dry out faster than one on the floor because it's closer to the ceiling, while a plant in a porous terracotta pot will use up water more readily than one in a non-porous plastic pot.

The problem with blanket watering advice is that none of these variables are being taken into consideration. How can you trust that a certain plant likes to be watered 'once a week' when nothing other than the regularity of watering is being considered? This type of care advice is better ignored. If your plant is in a shaded corner and you have been told it likes to be watered once a week, it's likely you will end up killing it because it doesn't have the intensity of light available to make

use of the water. The advice available on how to water your plant is problematic in many ways – take these examples I found online for watering a Swiss cheese plant:

'Water moderately and evenly about once a week'
'They like to dry out a little bit between waterings'
'Water thoroughly when the top soil is dry'
'Moderate levels of watering are required'

The advice used to describe how wet or dry the soil should be or how often to water it is subjective. What is 'moderate' to you will be different to me; what I take to mean 'dry' will be different for you. Every plant in our home has a different watering need, a one-size-fits-all approach will not work, so consider the advice to be a general guide and always check the soil before watering. This is the only way to get to know how fast a particular plant is using up the water you are giving it.

Does your plant need water?

I recommend using one of these methods before watering your plant:

— Push your finger into the soil as deep as it will go and feel for any moisture. I'm not a fan of the suggestion 'let the top inch of soil dry out and then water' – the top 5cm (2in) of soil may feel dry, but what if it's a large, deep pot? It may still be wet 15cm (6in) down, and pouring in more water would be a bad idea.
— Take a chopstick and push it deep into the soil, leave for a few minutes, then pull it out. If the chopstick comes out clean, the soil is dry.
— Weigh the pot in your hands. Picking up your plant (in its pot) and familiarising yourself with how heavy it feels after watering is an easy way to determine whether it needs water or not. If it feels very light, the soil is likely to be dry. If it feels heavy, there is still likely to be water in the soil and no need to add more. This method, although useful, only works when the plant is small, so don't go trying to pick up your giant fiddle leaf fig. A chopstick would be better for a plant in a large pot.
— Use your eyes to familiarise yourself with how the soil looks when it is both wet and dry.

There are other methods of working out when you should water, such as using a moisture meter, but this is not something I'd advocate using for a few reasons. For starters, why buy something that's made of plastic (which will eventually end up in landfill and pollute the planet for 500 years), when your finger is an eco-friendly and long-lasting alternative. Also, meters have been known to provide inaccurate readings.

I know you love your plant, or you wouldn't be reading this book, but there are other ways to show your love than through overzealous watering. Show you care by changing your watering habits – opt for checking the soil once a week, rather than watering once a week.

Many plants will forgive an occasional drought, but few can survive a lack of light and too much water. Often, a thirsty plant will give you an early warning sign that it needs a drink (some may curl their leaves inwards or droop), which can usually be quickly rectified. A plant that is drowning may only give you warning signs when it is already too late.

If you engage your senses, caring for your plant will become intuitive. I have hundreds of plants, which may sound like a daunting prospect when it comes to watering, and while it can be a little bit like spinning plates, it's never the case that they all need watering at the same time. I have come to instinctively know when I need to check the soil of each plant to see if it's thirsty. Using my eyes and hands every day is the only schedule I stick to when it comes to watering.

Type of water

If plants could speak, they'd likely say that they would like to be watered with rainwater. It contains fewer harmful chemicals than tap water, it's environmentally friendly and won't cost you a penny. However, having a good, constant supply of rainwater is dependent on where you live and whether you have a means of collecting it. I use a very sophisticated method of rainwater collection: buckets in the garden.

If you don't have a garden or live somewhere very arid, tap water is fine for most houseplants. Chlorine, fluoride, calcium, sodium and aluminium are often present in tap water, but not in high enough concentrations to cause a problem for plants. If you use water softening salts, this can cause a build-up of harmful minerals in the soil, so instead try to use rainwater whenever possible.

Carnivorous plants should never be watered with tap water – tap water is unsuitable because of the minerals and added chemicals. Dracaenas, calatheas and the spider plant can be sensitive to even low levels of dissolved chemicals in tap water, so keep a watchful eye on these plants – burnt, crispy leaf tips can be a symptom of excessive minerals.

Please don't buy bottled water for your plants: plastic is one of the biggest disasters our planet faces and we must avoid using it as much as we possibly can. We should also be mindful of conserving and reusing water whenever possible, and these are some options:

— If you have a freshwater aquarium (not saltwater), use the water you remove during a water change. I also soak my air plants and vanda orchid roots once a week in my home aquarium.
— Use water collected in a dehumidifier, reverse osmosis unit or tumble dryer.
— Bathwater is fine to use if no washing products have been added.
— Water used to boil vegetables or eggs can also be used, but let it cool first and don't use if salt has been added.

Temperature of water

The temperature of the water you use is not of great importance as long as it's not freezing cold. No harm has ever come to any of my plants by using cold water straight from the tap or rainwater from a bucket outside. Saying that, I would never use ice cubes to water my orchids, as some people recommend – melting ice could be harmful to the roots and it's not an effective way to evenly moisten the potting mix. It's far better to use the soaking method (see page 65).

General tips

— To make sure the water you give your plant stays in the pot, ensure the level of soil in the pot is about 5cm (2in) below the rim. This should allow you to water the plant without water rolling off the top of the soil, over the rim of the pot and down the sides.
— Where you decide to put your plant can have an impact on how often you water it. If it's at eye-level and easy to reach, you'll probably check the soil often and water when necessary. If you put it high up on a shelf, where it's a chore to access, it won't get watered as often and

may always be thirsty. The easier they are to reach, the more likely you are to give them the care they need (this paragraph is for you mounted staghorn fern).

— When watering your plants during the growing season, the aim is to fully saturate the potting mix. This ensures that all the roots are able to absorb water. Having said that, in winter, when most plants are using less water and the light and temperature are less intense than in summer, you might choose not to fully saturate the soil every time you water in order to reduce the risk of root rot (see Seasonal Changes on page 66).

— This one is a time-saving hack. If you have lots of plants, particularly small ones, sit them on a tray. That way, when you come to water them you can simply pick up the tray and take all your plants to the sink to water. I also have a metal shelving stand where I keep lots of plants – the shelves are made of mesh metal so when I pour water into the pots on the top shelf the water drains out of the bottom of the terracotta pots and onto the plants below. I have a drip tray on the floor under the shelves to collect any excess water.

The best way to water plants will always be a talking point because there is no right or wrong way, only the method that suits you. Don't stick with what you're used to or told to do, try new things, experiment with different watering styles, mix them up – that way, you'll find out what works best for you and your plants.

Watering from above

A common mistake is pouring water into the inner grow pot while it is still in its cover pot: the excess water has no means of escape and collects at the bottom causing the soil to become wet and root rot to develop. If it's a manageable size, take your plant out of the decorative cover pot and over to the sink. Using the tap (or a watering can), pour until the whole surface of the soil is saturated and you can see water dripping out of the bottom of the pot's drainage holes. Once the water has stopped dripping, replace the inner pot into its cover pot and move the plant back where it belongs. Large plants are best left in situ, sat on saucers, where you can see the excess water and pour it away. If the pot is too heavy to lift, suck up any excess water from the saucer using a turkey baster.

When watering from above be aware that there are a few types of plant that don't like water to pool on their leaves. Water doesn't roll off hairy leaves in the same way it does from smooth, glossy leaves, and if the water is left for a prolonged period, a damp leaf can become a breeding ground for fungal bacteria. Plants such as *Saxifraga stolonifera*, begonias and African violets are particularly susceptible to leaf fungal infections caused by excess moisture on their leaves, so I would suggest watering these from below.

Watering from below

To water from below, take the plant out of the cover pot and place it in a container or sink filled with a few inches of water. Leave the plant to soak up water for 15–30 minutes. You may choose to occasionally add fertiliser to the water during a plant's growing period.

Watering a plant from below allows the roots to take up as much water as the plant needs at that given time. While allowing your plant to quench its thirst sounds appealing to those who own a few plants, this method of watering isn't the most practical for those with more than a handful of plants as it is quite time-consuming.

Bear in mind, watering from below doesn't allow a build-up of salts and mineral deposits to be washed out of the soil. If this is your preferred method, water from above once in a while (ideally with rainwater) to help flush out a potentially harmful accumulation.

Soaking

A few plants enjoy a good soak, allowing them to access moisture for a longer period of time. Moth orchids potted in bark are a good example. Signs that a moth orchid is dehydrated include floppy or wrinkled leaves and brittle roots. Healthy roots should be plump and turn from silver to green when watered; if they are shrivelled and brown, they are rotten and should be removed.

You can soak your orchid without removing it from the decorative cover pot: simply pour water into the pot until it reaches the rim and leave it for 15–30 minutes. If it's not in a cover pot, take it to the sink or place it in a pot (without a drainage hole) and fill it up until the water almost reaches the rim. Take care not to let water sit on or over the crown of an orchid as it can cause it to rot. If you splash water on the crown, dry it off with a soft cloth.

Air plants also need a regular soak. There is a common misconception that air plants live on air alone: all plants need water and they are no exception. But unlike other plants they rely on their leaves, rather than roots, for water. Each plant will have a different way of expressing thirst so look out for small changes in appearance. Clues to when your air plant needs watering can include wrinkled leaves that feel papery rather than plump, or curled or drooping leaves.

There are a few methods that can be used to hydrate an air plant, including misting and soaking. Misting is giving your air plant a small drink, but it's not enough to completely satisfy its needs. To properly hydrate your plant, it will need to be soaked. When you soak an air plant it should be left for an hour or two completely submerged in water (preferably rainwater). After soaking, be sure to shake off the excess water so it doesn't rot the leaves, then set aside (ideally upside down) to fully dry before placing it back where it lives.

Seasonal changes and dormancy

Dormancy is a state of reduced metabolic activity and is triggered by environmental changes such as temperature, light and rainfall. For example, during autumn in the UK, the days get shorter and the temperature drops, and plants outside begin to prepare for dormancy in various ways, most commonly by discarding their leaves.

The seasons in many countries are well defined, but in regions with tropical or arid climates (where most of our houseplants originate), the temperature and weather conditions often remain more constant throughout the year and plants may never move into dormancy. Indoor plants experience a similarly constant environment, so dormancy won't necessarily occur, but you may notice some changes.

The light coming into our homes in winter is less intense than in summer and has a major impact on a plant's ability to photosynthesise. The plant is forced to try to adapt to the low levels of light, which can cause a stress reaction such as dropping leaves and loss of vigour. Plants that are better able to adapt to low-light conditions may keep growing regardless. Plants that have experienced poor care during the previous seasons – such as not enough light – may not have enough energy stored up to survive the reduction in light levels. The impact lower light levels have on our plants during winter illustrates perfectly why light is so vital to their health.

We lose more plants in winter than in summer and this, in most cases, is because they aren't getting enough light to use up the water in the soil. Think of it this way: you require more water to replenish your body during a run in summer than during a walk in winter. In the winter months, when the light and temperature are lower, most plants are metaphorically walking and require less water than if they were running (in their growing period). Reducing water in winter is necessary to balance the reduction in light, but if you have a plant that is growing new leaves during winter it will be using more water than those that aren't actively growing.

Watch closely to see how your plants are behaving: if they've stopped growing you must reduce watering (and stop fertilising). Keep checking the soil and make an informed judgement on when to water. As a very rough guide, I would suggest reducing how much you water by at least 50% during the winter period (unless your plants are growing). In winter I may water my foliage plants only once every two to three weeks, or in the case of cacti, once during the entire season. This may give you an idea of how much to reduce watering during winter, but remember to assess your particular plant's needs and the conditions you're providing.

Watering cacti and succulents

Cacti and succulents have adapted to deal with long periods of drought, so the assumption is that they don't need much water. This isn't true if they are getting bright light and warm temperatures through the spring and summer months. Cacti and succulents can and do like to be watered as regularly as foliage plants, but only if they are growing in a potting mix that drains quickly (such as one that contains 50–75% grit).

Cacti and succulents are opportunists and they have adapted to absorb water quickly when it becomes available. They are not used to water sitting around their roots because they are found in soils that are very free-draining. If the soil is too dense, moisture will remain near the roots for a prolonged period and can put them at risk of rotting. In summer, when temperatures increase and the days become brighter and longer, I put most of my cacti and some of my succulents outside so they can experience light from the sun, as nature intended. If you want to see impressive growth, put them outside – you will be amazed by how much better they grow outdoors and how much water they use.

When transitioning cacti and succulents from indoors to outdoors, it's important to do so gradually and after the risk of frost has completely passed. It's best to acclimatise them in spring when the sun isn't too intense. Start by putting them in a semi-shaded area for a few hours a day, then bring them back inside, keep increasing the amount of time you leave them outside, but never leave them in direct sun (which can cause scorching). After a few weeks you can start leaving them outside overnight. Keep an eye on the weather: if there is a period of rain forecast (which is very often the case in the UK), put your cacti where they won't get soaked.

When the temperature begins to drop at the end of the season, it's time to bring them back inside and overwinter them indoors. Before bringing them in, allow them to dry out as much as possible and check them over for pests or bugs. Place them in a bright position next to a window and reduce the amount of water you give them.

Aeration

Compacted soil occurs when the particles are pressed tightly together, making it difficult for the water to penetrate evenly. If water can't reach a plant's roots, then watering will be less effective. If the potting mix feels hard rather than crumbly, or water rolls off the surface rather than sinking in, it may be compacted and should be loosened and aerated.

In nature, worms and other insects help to keep oxygen, nutrients and water circulating in the soil. Indoors, we can mimic the worm by using a pencil or chopstick (or something similar) to loosen the potting mix.

A recent study found that roots may be able to sense soil compaction. Plant hormone ethylene diffuses through aerated soil, but compacted soil can cause a build-up of the hormone near root tissues, which in turn stop growing. If this is the case, not aerating your soil can also impede healthy root growth – another reason to get 'worming' or repotting in fresh soil.

Guttation

If you've ever noticed droplets of water at the tips of your plant's leaves, this is nothing to worry about – it's a natural process that the plant performs called guttation. During the day, moisture is released from the plant through the stomata (tiny openings in the plant tissue), but at night these 'pores' are closed. So at night, if the soil is moist, pressure builds up in the roots from the water absorbed and this pressure

pushes it up through the plant. To protect the leaf from being damaged, water is pushed out of pores called hydathodes (openings that are usually on the leaf margins), as these always remain open for this purpose. If you water your plants in the evening or keep them in self-watering pots, you may notice this happening more often than if you water plants during the day.

Guttation is performed to protect the leaves from becoming damaged by excess water, which can cause a disorder called oedema. Oedema is caused when roots take up water faster than the plant can use it or release it through transpiration. Cell damage can be very obvious on plants such as a fiddle leaf fig, which may show tiny brown dots, particularly on the undersides of the leaves. If you notice this, move your plant to a brighter location so the water can be used up more quickly.

While the process of guttation is not harmful to the plant, if you are overzealous with fertiliser, it can cause the tips of the plant to brown. The roots absorb water and minerals – if there is an excess of minerals in the soil, this will also be released through the openings on the leaf tips, where it can cause them to burn.

Monocot and dicot

Broadly speaking, plants can be divided into two types: flowering (angiosperms) and flowerless (gymnosperms). Based on the embryo in the seed, flowering plants are further divided into two categories: monocotyledons (or monocots) and dicotyledons (dicots).

A monocot will produce a single leaf from a seed, a dicot will produce two. Most monocots have a fibrous, web-like root system that tends to form nearer the surface of the soil, while most dicots have a large taproot from which smaller roots will branch. The main noticeable difference is in the leaf veins: monocot leaves have parallel veins, while dicots form branching veins from the central vein (midrib).

Although not visible to the naked eye, the distribution of stomata on the leaves also differs: monocots have stomata equally distributed on the surface and underside of the leaf, while dicots have few or no stomata on the top surface. All plants need their leaves to be kept free from dust; the stomata of monocots can be easily blocked by even a thin layer of dust, which can impact photosynthesis.

Interestingly, bulliform cells, found in the upper leaf epidermis of many monocots, have the ability to make the leaves curl when the plant is drought-stressed. This action reduces the surface exposure to sunlight and consequently helps to reduce water loss through transpiration.

The LAW

Here's where I lay down the LAW. I came up with this acronym of 'light and water' to illustrate the delicate balancing act you need to master. The light and water we give our plants must be evenly balanced. This really is the most important piece of care advice I can give and the most effective in preserving the health and longevity of your plants. It's simple to remember: what you add to one side of the scales you must add to the other to keep it balanced.

If you reduce light, reduce the amount of water. If you increase light, increase the amount of water. Tipping the scales on either side will result in a plant under stress. Too much water and not enough light will result in root rot, too little water and too much light can cause wilting.

Remember the LAW every time you go to water your plants. You shouldn't need to give a plant sitting far back from a window the same amount of water as one that sits beside a bright window.

If you take away nothing from this book other than the LAW of houseplants, then my job here is done. If you think of the LAW every time you pick up the watering can, I know that many plants' lives will be saved.

Temperature

Most foliage houseplants originate from regions with tropical climates and are therefore comfortable with the average daytime temperature of 18–21°C in our homes. Many will also tolerate much higher and lower temperatures, but some do not appreciate rapid fluctuations, especially cold or cold draughts. A plant that has happily existed in a hallway for most of the year could become stressed in winter when the front door is repeatedly opened and closed.

Temperature plays an important part in photosynthesis, so a cold draught will affect the rate the plant is able to photosynthesise. Higher temperatures (combined with longer durations or greater intensity of light) will increase the rate of photosynthesis, which in summer means your plants will need water more frequently than in winter. If the temperature becomes too high, the enzymes involved in the reaction breakdown and photosynthesis will stop (this will vary from plant to plant).

Many houseplants have evolved in environments that experience slightly cooler nighttime temperatures, so while a rapid change in temperature can cause serious trouble, normal fluctuations in day and nighttime temperatures aren't a cause for concern. In our thermostat-controlled homes, the average temperature doesn't change much regardless of the season – a drop or increase of 10°C is unlikely to cause harm. It's only if the temperature rises way above or dips well below average that there may be a problem.

In winter, check that the plants sitting next to windows aren't in a cold draught. If your hand feels cold, your plants will too and may appreciate being moved off the windowsill and onto a table pushed near to the window where they can still get the maximum amount of light without the draught. You can also use masking tape to seal any gaps around the windows – it's not attractive, but it is an option.

In summer, when the sun is at its most intense, the potting mix will need to be checked for moisture more frequently than in winter. Pay particular attention to those pots sitting on shelves or hanging from the ceiling. Warm air rises and therefore the soil in these pots can dry out more quickly than those on the floor.

Be aware of the damage central heating, open fires, stoves and air conditioning can cause to plants positioned close by to these sources. Blasting cold or hot air directly at the leaves of a plant can interfere with the process of photosynthesis and cause the health of the plant to suffer. Imagine how you'd feel sitting directly under or beside an air conditioning unit or fire all day long. What isn't comfortable for us, won't be comfortable for our plants. We can regulate our temperature by moving away, they cannot. Make any seasonal changes you need to ensure your plants are in the best possible positions all year around.

Humidity

Houseplants are plants that are able to adapt to an indoor environment. Many species originate from humid, tropical regions, but are happy to accept much lower humidity in our homes. If they couldn't adapt to the dry air in our homes, we would have realised this very early on and not bothered cultivating them for sale as houseplants. This is why the level of humidity in my house isn't something I ever lose sleep over – in other words, on the list of important things to try and get right for your houseplants, humidity ranks low.

Humidity plays a part in transpiration: when it's high, transpiration decreases; when it's low, transpiration increases. With this in mind, it makes sense that in winter, in our heated homes, our plants struggle with the dry air, but we can't blame the symptoms of an ailing plant on one aspect of the environment. Blaming a lack of humidity for brown leaf tips may not be entirely justifiable – it could play a part in the problem, but it's more likely your plant is suffering from a combination of light and water stress, rather than just low humidity. (See page 190 for other causes of brown leaf tips.)

An average home (apart from those in extremely cold or arid areas of the world) has a range of 30–60% humidity, which is perfectly adequate for the majority of houseplants. The humidity in my home hovers around the 35–40% mark in winter, so I tend not to worry about having to raise it. If the humidity is lower than about 25%, you may want to consider increasing it.

Advice on how to raise humidity effectively around indoor plants generally isn't very helpful. One of the most common suggestions is to pour water into a saucer filled with gravel and place the plant on top; another common tip is to mist your plant. This advice is not effective enough to make any major long-term difference to overall humidity in the room. Both methods might raise the humidity slightly, but not significantly and only for a short time. In the case of misting, it will only be effective for the few seconds it takes the water droplets to evaporate. Misting a plant with a spray bottle is pretty pointless if you are doing it to increase humidity, and could actually cause harm.

Plants have an outer waxy coating on their leaves called the cuticle. It is a protective layer with many important

functions, including repelling water to stop it being absorbed and diluting the sap within. Misting isn't really a beneficial activity for your plants and may increase the risk of bacterial and fungal infection, particularly to hairy-leafed plants such as African violets and begonias, which are susceptible to powdery mildew and fungal bacteria caused by moisture on the leaves.

Grouping a number of plants closely together is another common suggestion for raising humidity – I do this out of necessity (due to lack of space) rather than actively trying to increase the humidity. During transpiration, moisture is released from plant leaves, which can contribute to humidity levels – it seems like a small added bonus to bunching them together rather than a solution to raising the overall humidity. I like to believe plants can sense when they are near each other and could be communicating, but I suspect the most common topic of conversation is how hungry they are, rather than the lack of humidity in the room.

We're often told that bathrooms and kitchens are good places for plants that like humidity, but again, the humidity is only raised when the shower is on or the pan of pasta is boiling. When these stop, the humidity returns to the same level as any other room.

The most effective way of increasing humidity is to use a humidifier. There is a huge selection available, most are affordable and reasonably attractive. If you do want to use one, my advice would be to buy one that has a large capacity for holding water so you don't have to fill it up every few hours.

Supporting Growth

In their natural environment, plants have all they need to survive; bring them inside and they have nothing other than the pot and soil they arrived in. The health and happiness of our houseplants is dependent on us providing them with what they need, and the potting mix we choose is just as important as any other piece in the jigsaw. There are a baffling variety of ingredients you can use when potting up your plants and in this chapter you'll find suggestions for some of the most popular and lesser-known potting media, as well as what to do when your plant needs more room to grow.

Potting on – that is, moving a plant into a larger pot – is one of the aspects of growing plants that seems to induce fear, panic and many questions. How do I repot? When do I repot? How big should the pot be? Can you do it for me? Like it or not, plants grow out of their pots just as children grow out of clothes. There is nothing to fear, in fact, you should be congratulating yourself you've managed to keep your plant alive and it's actually growing. This is great news! It's a milestone! Whatever you've been doing, you've been doing it well, and if you'd like this happy, mutually beneficial relationship to continue, you must take the next step.

An often overlooked aspect of caring for plants is feeding them. Plants make their own food through photosynthesis, but without access to essential minerals and nutrients they can't grow strong and healthy and will lose vigour. Unlike plants in their natural habitat, where they can send out roots to search for what they need, houseplants are confined by their pot and are reliant upon us to provide them with these vital ingredients. Get your plant food right, and you'll be rewarded with strong, healthy growth.

Houseplant Soil

A plant needs water and nutrients, but it also needs oxygen around its roots to function; the texture of the houseplant soil you use has a major impact on the overall health of the plant. If you've baked a cake, you'll know that getting the right amount of each ingredient can mean the difference between a light and fluffy sponge or one so dense and heavy that it could be used as a weapon. The ingredients that make up houseplant soil (otherwise known as potting mix) can make it light and airy, meaning water travels quickly through it, or heavy and dense, meaning water will be retained for longer. If the mix is too light, your plant won't be supported to stand upright and water will pour from the bottom of the pot as quickly as you pour it in, which will leave the roots thirsty. If the mix is too heavy, the water will stay in the soil, potentially making it anaerobic. Aerobic soil allows for free movement of air; anaerobic soil leaves the air flow and oxygen restricted, which is a potential killer for plants. Anaerobic soil and water leads to root rot, and without roots the plant will die.

So how do you decide which soil your plant needs and which ingredients to choose to create the right mix? As always, you should start by finding out where your plant originates from in the wild, as this will give you the biggest clue to the potting mix it prefers: if it comes from the forest floor, it's likely to thrive in a soil rich in decomposed organic matter; if it comes from an arid, desert environment, it's likely to prefer something gritty that drains quickly; and if it grows on trees (as epiphytes do), it would probably prefer a chunky soil made predominantly from bark. The majority of indoor plants prefer a soil with a mixture of large and small particles, but do some research into your plant's origins before deciding on the ingredients in your potting mix.

Buying premixed houseplant soil is convenient but expensive, so why not make your own recipe, choosing ingredients from those listed in this chapter, or experiment with other substrates (of which there are many). The only no-nos are digging up soil from outside (as it may carry pests and disease), and buying a potting mix that has a devastating environmental impact (more on this on the next page). It's worth noting that most things we use for our plants, in one way or another, have a detrimental effect on the environment.

Say no to peat

For many years, peat has been one of the most popular potting media. Made partly from decomposed sphagnum moss together with other organic matter from bogs, it has for decades been a staple compost for outdoor and indoor gardeners. But this must stop. Not only is peat a non-renewable resource (1mm of peat takes a year to form), peat bogs are also a major player in the fight against climate change due to their incredible ability to lock in and store carbon. A peat bog can hold up to ten times more carbon per hectare than a forest, and globally peatlands store half a trillion tonnes of carbon. When peat is extracted, these superpowers are reversed and instead of locking away carbon, the bog releases it into the atmosphere.

Peatlands are also home to a wide variety of animals, plants and insects and are one of the most threatened ecosystems on Earth. Some peat producers will make persuasive arguments about how they are managing the bogs in a sustainable way, restoring and reseeding them with moss, but once they have been pillaged they will never return to their former glory. Degrading and destroying peat bogs also makes the land more vulnerable to severe wildfires.

Thankfully, many manufacturers are now making peat-free alternatives and the UK government will ban sales of peat compost for use in horticulture by 2024, which is a recognition of the problem, but it doesn't go far enough. Imported potted plants grown in peat are not currently covered by this ban. Many industry experts, including Monty Don, have expressed their support for an urgent ban on extracting peat, which Don describes as 'environmental vandalism'.

Let's do our bit to keep peat and peat moss out of our pots and leave them in the ground where they belong. Ask questions, do some research into the brand and their ethics before buying sphagnum moss or potting mix. Sphagnum moss is grown predominantly on peatlands and any claims of 'sustainability' do not necessarily negate the issue that a precious ecosystem is being exploited.

Houseplant soil that has been premixed

If you don't have time to make up your own potting mix or you're not sure what to use, your best bet would be to opt for a premixed, branded houseplant soil that can be used for all plants with the exception of cacti and succulents, as these require more drainage. Premixed houseplant soil will usually

contain a combination of compost (green waste and bark), loam (sand and silt), coir and clay granules. Always check the label and avoid buying it if it contains peat or sphagnum moss.

Compost

Compost is simply decayed organic matter. It can be made at home in a compost bin or bought in bags. Small amounts of the compost you make at home can be added to other potting media in a houseplant potting mix. Compost can also describe a potting mix that's created to a specific recipe – it can be bought in bags and can contain a variety of media including bark, coconut husk, rockwool, sand, grit, perlite and green garden waste. Labelling is often vague, so always make sure the compost you are buying doesn't contain peat.

Coconut coir

Coir is produced from coconut husks and is regarded as an alternative to peat, though it still has environmental drawbacks. Its water-holding ability is particularly useful, while at the same time it allows for good drainage and aeration. Coir is relatively inexpensive compared to perlite or vermiculite and can be bought as bricks, which when soaked in water expand to more than double the size.

Coir is becoming a popular alternative for commercial growers who historically have used peat, but be aware that it contains very few nutrients, so if you buy a plant that is potted only in coir, it will need feeding or repotting a few weeks after arriving in your home.

The downsides of using coir are that it's very light, it can work its way up to the surface of the soil and it may not hold your plant upright if you add a lot of it into the potting mix. It's also high in salts, which can lead to a build-up in the houseplant soil. Despite its downsides, it remains an option if you don't want to use peat.

Coir is a byproduct of the coconut industry, but you can't ignore the vast swathes of rainforest that have been cleared to make way for coconut farming. It's also worth noting that a significant amount of water is used to clean coir of salts, and the runoff has been known to end up in rivers. Concerns have also been raised about the pay and conditions of employees working to process coir. Primarily produced in countries including Sri Lanka, Philippines, Indonesia and Mexico, coir is often imported by air freight, which of course contributes to CO_2 emissions. There have been reports of abuse suffered by monkeys forced to collect coconuts on some farms in Thailand, so do some research on the product you're buying.

Perlite

When you buy a potted plant from a shop, you may find small white particles in the potting mix – these are often mistaken for polystyrene or even mealybugs, but in fact they are perlite.

Perlite is formed when molten rock expelled from volcanoes rapidly cools, trapping water within the rock to form a glass-like structure. It is extracted and then heated to an extremely high temperature until the particles pop, like popcorn, and turn white.

It is predominantly used in a potting mix to improve aeration by keeping the soil from compacting and aiding drainage. There is limited unbiased information available about the environmental impact of using perlite, but it's worth noting that it is mined (from open cast mines) and it is a mineral, therefore there is a finite amount available.

Vermiculite

Comparisons are often made between perlite and vermiculite. Vermiculite is similarly a mined rock product (that's also non-renewable), and is extracted and then heated at extreme temperatures in order to cause the particles to expand. It's used to improve aeration in a potting mix, while also being water retentive (unlike perlite, which does not hold water). Vermiculite is best used for plants that don't like the soil to totally dry out between watering, whereas perlite is a good choice for plants that require the soil to totally dry out between watering.

Rice hulls

Rice hulls are the outer husks of grains of rice that are removed after harvesting. Like coconut coir, they are a byproduct and would otherwise be wasted. Using them in a potting mix gives them a new purpose, aiding aeration and allowing good drainage. They are useful as an alternative to perlite and to improve the texture of a potting mix. The rice hulls decompose in the soil so will need to be replaced after a year or so.

Biochar (horticultural charcoal)

Biochar is a charcoal-like substance made from waste wood and agricultural byproducts that would otherwise be sent to landfill. The process of burning in a low-oxygen environment captures the carbon absorbed by the organic matter and converts it into a stable form, which means it won't end up in the atmosphere.

It's a porous substance so it can be added to soil to make it less compacted and more free-draining, while also increasing water and nutrient retention. The numerous benefits of biochar make it a good option when making your own potting mix.

Pumice

An increasingly popular ingredient, pumice is used in a potting mix to create a light, airy, free-draining texture particularly suitable for cacti and succulents. It has the benefit of being heavier than perlite, so it won't work its way to the top of the soil, but it is less readily available and more expensive.

Pumice is a volcanic rock formed when lava cools, trapping gas bubbles in the process. Pumice mining is considered more environmentally friendly than many other mineral extractions. This is mainly due to the nature of how pumice is formed, deposited on the surface of the earth, rather than deep underground.

Sand and grit

Sand and grit (often labelled as grit sand or sand/grit), are a variety of different types of stone crushed to a certain size. When buying sand make sure it is horticultural sand and not builders' or play sand, as those are made up of smaller particles that can become compacted. Horticultural sand improves aeration and drainage and is a good addition in a potting mix for cacti and succulents.

As with everything humans extract from the earth, there is a negative environmental impact – mining takes place across the world and sand and grit are dug from pits, dredged from riverbeds and scooped up from the seabed. However, the vast majority of sand is used in the building industry, not the horticultural industry.

Bark

Bark is a byproduct of the timber industry. Adding it to a potting mix improves aeration and drainage. If the bark is finely milled it can be a good substitute for peat. Larger chunks can be added for an airier, more free-draining mix.

Leca

Hydroculture (or hydroponics) is becoming an increasingly popular way to grow houseplants and involves growing plants in the soil-free medium of water. Leca is a semi-hydro system – the lightweight, baked clay balls absorb water, allowing the roots to access it by using a wicking process.

As with all media there are pros and cons: leca doesn't provide the plants with any nutrients, so you must add fertiliser, but on the plus side, the medium is reusable and it also reduces the risk of houseplant pests and makes dealing with them easier.

Before you rush off to repot all your plants into leca, you might need to give it a bit more thought: there are people who swear by only using leca for their plants and others who have tried it and would never use it again. It may produce good results in the short term, but I do wonder about its long-term impact on a plant.

Cat litter

Cat litter can be used as a more cost-effective alternative to vermiculite and as a partial substitute for expensive Akadama bonsai potting media. If you are adding it to your potting mix, make sure to buy clay-based, non-clumping litter, as well as a low-dust variety. I've added it to a houseplant soil when making kokedama as it helps hold the shape of the ball. It is also used by some cacti and succulent growers.

Vermicast or worm castings

Vermicast is organic matter processed by worms – what comes out (after it's been through the body of the worm), is worm manure. It's an incredible, natural fertiliser due to its exceptionally high levels of soluble minerals and nutrients. Unlike pre-packaged, artificial chemical fertilisers, which are a bit like plant junk food, vermicast is organic, natural and releases nutrients slowly.

Pots

Pots come in many shapes and sizes, and it's useful to get a handle on a few basics.

Grow/inner pot

This is the (typically) plastic pot that your plant comes in when you buy it. It has drainage holes at the bottom. Many people use this grow pot as an inner pot, slotting it into a decorative pot.

Decorative/outer pot

This is an attractive pot that is used to conceal a grow pot. It may or may not have a drainage hole. If it has a drainage hole, the plant can be planted directly into the decorative pot, but you will need a tray below to collect excess water.

Drainage

When it comes to drainage holes, my advice would be to choose a pot with a hole or a few holes. This allows the water that is poured into the pot to escape through the bottom. Without any holes, excess water that your plant doesn't use will remain at the bottom of the pot and encourage root rot. Roots need oxygen, and too much water reduces oxygen in the soil, which in turn increases bacteria and will eventually cause the roots to decay. Without a functioning root system, the plant will die.

Choose a pot with a drainage hole and you'll reduce the likelihood of waterlogged soil. That's not to say that there aren't people who have successfully kept plants alive in a pot without a drainage hole, but as a new plant owner, or one who has a history of killing plants, this isn't a good idea. Figuring out the right amount of water to give a plant is a balancing act and frankly there are enough things to think about without adding a lack of drainage to the list of potential problems.

Porous and non-porous pots

There are two types of pot material that you can choose for your plants: porous and non-porous.

A pot made from a porous material (such as terracotta, which is a traditional pot material) means that water can be absorbed by the pot itself. This can make it a particularly good choice for plants that prefer a drier soil, such as cacti and succulents. It is also a good choice for those houseplant enthusiasts who have a tendency to show their love through excessive watering.

The benefits of using a porous pot are:
— You can plant straight into it without an inner pot, though do make sure it has a drainage hole.
— They are inexpensive compared to many decorative pots.
— Most have a drainage hole and come with a saucer that can sit below.
— They allow water and air to move through the pot.
— They absorb water, reducing the risk of root rot.

There are also a few downsides:
— The soil dries out more quickly, so you may need to water more often.
— You can't place them directly onto a wooden surface without a saucer.
— They are easily broken.

The plants we buy usually come in plastic grow pots. Plastic is strong, flexible and light, but unlike terracotta, it isn't porous. Plastic pots hold moisture rather than wicking it away.

The benefits of using plastic pots are:
— They retain moisture, reducing watering frequency.
— They are durable and lightweight.
— They can be slotted into a decorative cover pot that doesn't have a drainage hole.

There are also a few downsides:
— It is easier to overwater your plant as excess water cannot be absorbed by plastic.
— They have very limited aesthetic appeal.
— The production of plastic pots – and the lack of recycling opportunities – is a disaster for the environment.

Plastic pots revolutionised the ability of growers to transport plants all over the world due to their lightweight quality compared to terracotta pots, but little progress has been made in manufacturing a viable, environmentally friendly alternative. A huge amount of plastic is being used by growers, not only in the pots, but also in the wrapping for transportation. Billions of plastic pots are in circulation throughout the world, with a high percentage ending up in landfill because most aren't recyclable – it makes the

seemingly green hobby of gardening anything but. Without a doubt, more needs to be done about the amount of plastic the gardening industry uses, and you can help drive the effort by asking your local garden centre about the steps they are taking to reduce their use of plastic and about the availability of alternatives. Many garden centres also offer a recycling service, so look out for this or ask for one to be introduced.

Self-watering pots

If you are forgetful, time poor, travel a lot, or don't trust yourself with watering, a self-watering pot may be the best option for you. The benefits of a self-watering pot are that it allows the plant continual access to water, which can be used at the rate the plant requires. All you have to do is fill up the reservoir and the plant will do the rest.

At the bottom (or to the side) of the main pot is a compartment that holds water – a cord is inserted in the pot's planting area that leads to the water reservoir and acts as a wick for the roots to draw up water. The amount of light the plant is receiving will have an impact on how regularly the reservoir will need topping up – this might be once every few weeks or once every few months.

I find that self-watering pots are good for plants that don't like the soil to become completely dry, such as ferns. I was given a maidenhair fern to rescue and tried for months to make it happy; it wasn't until I tried it in a self-watering pot and placed it in moderate to bright light that it flourished. Self-watering pots take away the element of guesswork when it comes to watering – find the sweet spot when it comes to light and you have the perfect combination for a plant to thrive. The downside of self-watering planters is they are more expensive than a normal pot, so instead of buying one you could have a go at making your own by repurposing an existing plastic bottle (see page 89 for a picture of this).

— Cut a plastic bottle in half and take the cap off.
— Fill the bottom section with water.
— Turn the top section upside down and insert it into the bottom section. The water should come no higher than the neck of the bottle.
— Feed a piece of cord through the neck of the bottle so that half is in the top section and half is in the water.
— Fill the top section with soil and add the plant.

Potting On and Repotting

'Potting on' describes removing your plant from its pot and replanting it in a pot that's at least one size larger than its current pot. 'Repotting' describes removing your plant from its pot, removing most of the old soil and then replacing it in the same pot with fresh potting mix.

Potting on is necessary for a growing plant. As the plant grows above the soil, so do its roots within the pot. Potting mix serves as the main source of water, nutrients and minerals for the majority of houseplants, so when the pot becomes too small for the roots, the amount of soil won't be enough to provide the roots with the elements it needs for healthy growth. A plant in nature sends out roots in search of water and nutrients, the instinct to do this isn't switched off when it's in a pot. All plants whose roots have outgrown the pot (even though there may be no visible signs of unhappiness), will be under a certain degree of stress and will benefit from being potted on into a larger pot.

There is advice that suggests some plants prefer to be potbound or rootbound, here is a list of a few I found on the internet: peace lily, spider plant, African violet, umbrella tree, ficus, agapanthus, asparagus fern, snake plant and Boston fern. I'm not sure when or to whom these plants spoke to about wanting to have their roots permanently and severely restricted, or why they have been singled out, but I suspect somewhere along the line the suggestion that these plants 'don't like to be in a pot that is too big' has been confused with 'likes to be rootbound'. The primary function of the roots of these plants is no different from any other plant, so why would they 'like' to have these restrictions placed on them? Speaking on behalf of the above plants, please can we remove them from the list and treat them as we would our other plants: when they show signs of needing more room to grow, pot them on into a bigger pot.

Pot size

While the reason for potting on is to give the roots more room, it's not a good idea to get the biggest pot you can find and move your plant into it. A small plant in a large pot will need longer to absorb water from the soil compared to a large plant in a small pot, and this increases the risk of the soil staying wet for a prolonged period of time, which can lead to root rot.

Many experts agree that you should only repot your plant into a pot that's one or two sizes bigger than the current one, but you can use this as a guide rather than a rule. The important thing is to give your plant an appropriate amount of water, and not so much that it ends up sitting in soggy soil surrounded
by water it can't absorb.

Signs you need to pot on

If you suspect your plant has grown out of its space, look out for these signs.
— Roots growing out of the bottom of the drainage holes.
— Growth has slowed or stopped.
— Yellow, brown or wilting leaves (usually the lower ones).
— The plant looks too big for the size of the pot.
— The pot is distorting out of shape.
— Water is flowing out of the bottom of the pot as soon as you pour it in.

Before concluding that the plant needs to move into a larger pot, it's best to investigate further by taking a look at the roots themselves. Tip the pot sideways and slide the plant out gently. If the roots are tightly circled around the base of the pot it's time to replace the current pot with a bigger one.

Some plants are better than others at letting you know when they need a new pot. The ZZ plant and snake plant will split a pot open with their expanding rhizomes (underground stems). These plants won't give you subtle hints when they would like a new pot, they will just bust out and demand a new home. If you see the plant distorting its pot shape, this is the rhizomes trying to find more room to grow. Using scissors to cut a pot open isn't usually necessary under normal circumstances, but depending on how distorted the pot has become, you may need to do this to get the plant out.

Signs you need to repot

If your plant doesn't need to be moved into a larger pot, it may benefit from being repotted into its existing pot with fresh soil. Look out for these signs before deciding whether to repot.

— Water is flowing out of the bottom of the pot as soon as you pour it in.
— Water is sitting on the surface of the soil and taking a long time to be absorbed.

- A gap has developed between the soil and the pot.
- The plant has been in the same soil for a few years.
- The plant has suffered from root rot.
- There is evidence of pests or mould on the surface.

When to pot on or repot

The most common suggestion, and potentially the best time to pot on or repot a plant, is spring, as this coincides with the beginning of a plant's active growing phase. However, the internet is a marvellous place to worry yourself stupid, particularly when it comes to dos and don'ts of houseplant care. A quick glance at a few websites can leave you crying in the corner wondering when your plant will die because you potted it on in the wrong season.

My attitude to repotting or potting on is that it should be done when the plant looks like it needs it. Don't sit back and watch an ailing plant struggling in a pot that is clearly too small, waiting for spring to come around. I wouldn't suggest repotting a plant that was in flower, but other than that, in my experience the month or season you repot isn't of great importance. If a plant's appearance changes, don't ignore the warning signs.

How to pot on or repot

The simplest way to pot on (or repot) is to follow these steps:

1. Hold your hand flat and slot the stem in between your fingers so that your palm covers the soil. If you are repotting cacti use gloves or encircle it with a band formed of newspaper or cardboard.
2. Tip the plant sideways and gently squeeze the pot all the way around. With your hand still across the surface of the pot, turn the pot upside down and the plant should release into your hand.
3. If the pot isn't made of plastic, tip it sideways and rest it on the floor. Use a small trowel or blunt knife to loosen the soil away from the sides of the pot and gently pull the plant out by the stem.
4. Gently loosen the roots so they aren't bound tightly together and remove some of the old soil, roughly two thirds. You don't need to remove all of the soil – this only needs to be done if you are treating pests or root rot.
5. Press enough soil into the bottom of the new pot so that when you place the plant in, the stem sits about 5cm

(2in) below the rim. It's important to leave space between the soil surface and top of the pot, to allow you to water the plant.

6. Fill in around the sides with fresh soil, tapping the pot on a hard surface and pressing the soil down gently.
7. Cover the surface with 1–2cm (½in) of fresh soil and press down gently.
8. Water to settle the soil.

A natural fungicide

If you are transplanting your plant because of root rot, this is a great time to treat it to a natural fungicide. Chamomile flowers are a natural source of sulphur, and sulphur is a fungicide that can help reduce the pathogens present in the soil and prevalent in the case of root rot.

After cutting off the roots damaged by rot, use a cooled cup of chamomile tea to rinse the remaining roots to help prevent them becoming infected.

Chamomile-infused water is also a great treatment for mould in a terrarium. Cut off affected leaves and use a misting bottle to spray a small amount of the solution onto the area.

Aftercare

We don't immediately relax and feel at home when we move to a new house, it takes time to settle in – this experience is the same for a plant in new soil. Plants adapt to changes, but while they're adapting, they might show signs of stress. If you notice some leaves falling off or the plant wilting after being transplanted, it could be suffering from shock. Some plants are more sensitive than others to this sort of change, particularly those that are already unhealthy.

If you notice changes in the appearance of a plant, try not to panic: the worst thing you can do is fuss over it, giving it yet more water, or moving it to different areas of the house in an attempt to help it perk up. Moving it to another area with different light intensity can add further stress.

After potting on or repotting a plant, try to keep everything else the same by placing it back in the spot it came from. Keep an eye on it but keep your hands off. If the plant was healthy before it was repotted it will likely perk up again after the roots have settled. An unhealthy plant that was already stressed before being moved into a new pot will be less likely to bounce back quickly, but that's not to say it won't. Check it has water, the right amount of light and warmth, and then leave it to recuperate.

A large plant that has been in the same pot for years could benefit from being repotted, which is easier said than done if the plant and pot are too heavy to move. Refreshing the top layer of soil is the next best thing to repotting and helps add vital nutrients and minerals that may have depleted over time. Top dressing alleviates the symptoms of a plant that needs repotting for a short period of time, but signs it needs an upgrade will begin to show again.

Top dressing can be done as often as you feel is necessary, it's easy to do and doesn't risk disturbing the roots. But the downside is the roots aren't being provided with extra space to grow. If moving the plant to a larger pot isn't an option, make sure to keep the plant well fed either by adding a slow-release fertiliser or top dressing a few times each year.

1. Use your fingers, a spoon or small trowel to remove the top few inches of soil – you can keep going until you see the top of the root ball. If the soil is very compacted, you may have to add some water first to help loosen it.
2. Aerate the remaining soil with a chopstick (see Aeration page 69).
3. Add fresh potting mix to refill the pot to about 5cm (2in) below the rim.
4. Water to settle the soil.

Plant Food

Light, water and roughly 20 other additional ingredients – referred to as macronutrients and micronutrients – are necessary for a plant to be able to create a meal of glucose and starch that's necessary for growth.

Macronutrients are required in large quantities and include carbon, hydrogen, oxygen, nitrogen, phosphorous, potassium, calcium, magnesium and sulphur.

Micronutrients are required in smaller quantities and include iron, manganese, boron, molybdenum, copper, zinc, chlorine, nickel, cobalt, sodium and silicon.

Plants get the first three of those macronutrients from the air and water, with the remaining ingredients found in the soil. Over time the soil is depleted of these nutrients and must be replaced if the plant is to remain healthy. Nitrogen, phosphorus and potassium are usually the ones that are depleted first because they are used in the largest amounts by the plant. Here is a very simplified explanation of how a plant uses each of these elements:

— Nitrogen helps foliage growth and chlorophyll production.
— Phosphorus assists the growth of roots.
— Potassium encourages flowering and is used to build strength and disease resistance.

Fertiliser

Most general plant fertilisers contain N (nitrogen), P (phosphorous) and K (potassium or potash) in varying ratios. In a general multipurpose fertiliser labelled 20-20-20, the elements are even (1 part N, 1 part P and 1 part K). Fertilisers labeled as 10-10-10 or 5-5-5 are the same ratio, just more diluted. If you have a flowering plant, you may want to choose a fertiliser that has more potassium, and for green foliage plants, you may choose one with more nitrogen.

The starting point for choosing a fertiliser for your plant is knowing which species you have. There are supplementary feeds targeted towards many different plants, such as cacti and succulents, flowering plants, citrus and so on, and these contain NPK in suitable ratios. This isn't to say that you must only buy fertiliser that is specifically created for a particular species of plant – you can use a general all-purpose feed on all of them. But just bear in mind that cacti and succulents require less fertiliser than foliage plants as they are adapted to poor-nutrient soils and can be happy for months without additional fertiliser.

Personally, I like adding seaweed as a tonic for my plants. It's natural, organic, sustainable and provides a vast array of essential nutrients. It can be purchased in liquid or dried form and from most garden centres or online. Some sources are more sustainable and renewable than others, so do your research before deciding which brand to buy.

Feeding a plant doesn't have to mean pouring in a fertiliser, you may also choose to add soil improvers. Adding a scoop of slow-release fertiliser to the bottom portion of a potting mix can be very effective. You can combine this with regular aeration of soil (using a chopstick) and then sporadically top dress (see page 97) with fresh houseplant soil that contains minerals (vermicast is a good addition). Once you top dress the plant, you won't need to worry about feeding again for at least a few months.

When to feed

How and when to feed your plant is determined by many factors, such as the type of plant, how much light it's receiving, the temperature, whether it's actively growing and the soil it's in. The reason we feed plants is so they can make food through photosynthesis. If the plant isn't growing, for example if it's positioned in low light, it won't need fertilising. Resting or dormant plants (i.e. those that are not actively growing) need much less water and don't need fertilising. If your plant is showing signs of nutrient deficiencies (see page 174), consider feeding.

I feed my cacti and succulents two to three times a year in the spring/summer period, whereas I feed my foliage plants approximately once a month (if they are growing). There are no rules I can give you to follow about how often to feed your own plants, as this will be down to your observations and based on the factors mentioned above, but as a general guide, if it's growing (and there is visible growth, such as new leaves) your plant needs feeding.

Remember that feeding an indoor plant is different to fertilising plants outdoors. In the garden, the fertiliser can leach away with rainwater and disperse through the soil, but this isn't the case for a plant imprisoned in a pot. So always follow the instructions on the fertiliser for the correct dosage: providing too much fertiliser can cause damage to many parts of the plants (see page 192 for symptoms of a build-up of minerals in the soil).

Houseplants for Your Home

Whether purchased on a whim or bought after weeks of deliberation, there is something undeniably exciting about a plant that's new to your home. If this initial sense of happiness is to continue, then choosing the right place for your plant is essential. I can't stress enough the importance of placing the new plant in a position where it will get the light it needs in order to feed itself through photosynthesis (see page 38). A plant with insufficient light can never reach its full potential as it will always be hungry and more likely to suffer from ailments. No one wants happiness to be replaced by frustration and disappointment.

When we buy plants, they have often come from nurseries where they've been basking in the optimum environment and where they've been receiving good light, warmth, water, humidity and fertiliser. This means they've been able to grow strong and healthy, while also storing food in reserve. A plant can dip into its food store when it gets hungry, but eventually the reserve will be depleted, and the plant won't have enough food to survive. The only way for the plant to make more food is by being in the right light conditions so it can photosynthesise.

The intensity of light plants need to be able to grow varies from species to species, but all plants require some light. There are plants that are better suited to low light areas of your home, and some that are better able to adapt to lower light levels than others – if they had the choice, these plants would file a request to be moved. Many plants that we are led to believe are 'good for low light areas' are actually just plants that are able to adapt, and it does not mean that they enjoy receiving the minimal amount of light possible for survival – they will just suffer in silence, hungry and dreaming of sunlight.

A great deal of money, not to mention numerous plant lives, could be saved if we put the basic requirements of the plant above the desire to make our room look nice. We may have what we consider 'the perfect spot' for a plant, but is it really perfect for that particular plant? This chapter should help you to find out.

| Water | In the advice on the following pages, you'll see some recurring terms to help you identify when you need to water your plant. But for more comprehensive advice, see page 58. To test for these types of moisture, use your finger, a chopstick or weigh the pot in your hands. |

Completely dry There is no moisture in the soil at all.
Approaching dry The soil will feel mostly dry. A slight coldness in the soil can be indicative of the last remnants of moisture, which I would describe as approaching dry.

| Light | The guidance I give on light and plant positioning is based on conditions during summer in the Northern Hemisphere. Do make sure that you translate the advice so that it is relevant to where you live in the world. For more on window direction, see page 47. |

| Size at maturity | I've included a rough guide to the mature size of each plant. When choosing a plant, it's good to consider how large it may eventually grow so you know in advance if you have adequate space. I've categorised them by height (which translates as length for trailing plants). |

Small Up to 30cm (1ft)
Medium Between 30cm–1.2m (1–4ft)
Large Over 1.2m (4ft)

| Feed | I have given a rough idea of how often and how much to feed a particular plant. I often suggest diluting liquid fertiliser to half the suggested strength on the bottle, this is to avoid potentially damaging the roots, which can be 'burnt' by excessive minerals. |

| Propagate | The majority of plants mentioned can be easily propagated. I've included which type of propagation method might yield success. Refer to page 228 for further details on how to grow a new plant from the parent plant. |

| Pets | Plant lovers are often also pet lovers, but the two don't always live in harmony. Certain plants are considered toxic to pets if ingested, which is why I've included their toxicity in the following profiles. Despite having three cats and a dog, I don't |

tend to worry about having plants that are considered toxic because none of them have ever shown an interest in chewing on them. The only issue I have is with them knocking the plants over. Don't despair if some of the plants you want to grow are considered toxic – you could always hang them up out of harm's way. Ultimately, you know your animals: if you think it's likely they'll be interested in taking a bite out of a plant, don't risk bringing it home, it's not worth it.

Easy/difficult

I don't describe plants as 'hard to kill' or 'easy care'. These phrases are the opposite of helpful, and can cause anxiety and stress for those whose home environments just aren't suitable for a particular plant. It's not helpful for a plant to be labelled 'easy' when you've killed three, as this only serves to undermine confidence. I can guarantee that a plant you find 'hard to kill' can currently be found on someone else's compost heap.

Sleeping with plants

A question I'm often asked is: 'is it okay to have plants in the bedroom'. There is a misconception that because plants emit CO_2, they can cause dangerous levels to accumulate in the room while we sleep. The very small level of CO_2 plants emit during the night is far less than the person/or animal you share a room with. Unless you are going to pack so many plants into your room that there is no longer space for a bed, I really wouldn't give the matter another thought. Plants are to be enjoyed in all rooms, apart from those without light. Why not buy a prayer plant and watch it lift its leaves from the comfort of your bed (see page 111).

Low Light

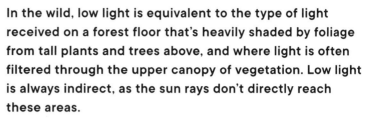

In the wild, low light is equivalent to the type of light received on a forest floor that's heavily shaded by foliage from tall plants and trees above, and where light is often filtered through the upper canopy of vegetation. Low light is always indirect, as the sun rays don't directly reach these areas.

At home, low light translates to a position close to a north-facing window (see page 47) or any area that's no further than 1.5–2m (5–6.5ft) from a window facing in any other direction. Further back than 2m would be considered deep shade. You'll need to move all plants closer to the windows in winter as the hours and intensity of daylight are reduced.

I want to apologise to almost all of these plants for adding them to this list. Unfortunately for them, their ability to adapt to almost any light condition has given them a reputation for being suited to the darkest corners of our homes. While there is truth in the fact that they can survive in low light, many of them would prefer to be closer to a window. If after a few months in low light your plant appears to be declining in health, experiment by putting it nearer to a window and see if it improves. When they are given moderate to bright light, some of them will grow more quickly, reproduce more readily and may even flower. Positioned in very low light, they might survive, but probably won't thrive. These are the silent sufferers of the plant world.

A note on ferns

Contrary to most houseplant books, I haven't included ferns in the low-light category. In my experience, they do better in moderate to bright light and some species even do well being placed under a grow light (my maidenhair fern has been doing particularly well under a grow light). I recommend using a self-watering pot if you move your fern to a bright spot or under a grow light – they need constant access to water and won't tolerate their soil completely drying out.

Weeping fig 'Variegata'
Ficus benjamina 'Variegata'

Family Moraceae

The weeping fig is indigenous to southern Asia and northern Australia. Its popularity as a houseplant can be attributed to its graceful appearance (the common name reflects its pendant branches that arch downwards), as well as its ability to adapt to low-light conditions. Numerous cultivars are available, offering different variations of leaf colour and pattern, including this variegated one. The sap contains latex, so avoid this plant if you have an allergy.

Tip *Sensitive to changes in its environment, particularly light, so find it a good spot and leave it alone. Environmental changes can result in leaf drop – should this happen, don't fuss, simply give it time to adjust and regrow new leaves. Leaf drop may also be caused by other problems (see page 199).*

Water Water when the soil is approaching dry. Check soil every 5–7 days in summer and every 10–12 days in winter

Light Position close to a north-facing window or no further than 2m (6.5ft) from an east-, west- or south-facing window. Would prefer moderate to bright light, but will tolerate a low light area

Soil General houseplant soil

Size at maturity Large

Feed Once a month during spring and summer, but dilute to half the suggested strength

Propagate Stem cutting

Pets Toxic

Jewel orchid
Ludisia discolor

Family Orchidaceae

This orchid is beloved for its beautiful foliage – its dark green or burgundy leaves with pink-red coloured stripes look hand painted. It's native to areas in southern Asia, where, unlike many other orchids, it grows on the forest floor rather than on trees.

Tip *I grow mine under a cloche and they also do well in terrariums.*

Water Prefers not to dry out completely, this does not mean it likes to sit in soggy soil. Let the soil approach dry before watering. Check soil every 5–7 days in summer and every 7–10 days in winter

Light This orchid is accepting of low light, but would appreciate the occasional hour or two of moderate to bright indirect light; it's likely to flower in a brighter location. Position close to a north-facing window or within 2m (6.5ft) of an east-, west- or south-facing window (move it closer to encourage flowering)

Soil Jewel orchids shouldn't be grown in orchid bark; a general houseplant soil is fine with the addition of a potting medium that aids aeration

Size at maturity Small

Feed Once a month in spring and summer, but dilute to half the suggested strength

Propagate Stem cutting

Pets Non-toxic

Ponytail palm / Elephant's foot
Beaucarnea recurvata

Family Asparagaceae

Despite its common name, the ponytail palm isn't a palm or a tree. Indigenous to Mexico, it is related to succulents like agave and yucca and it stores water in a bulbous caudex, making it well adapted to periods of drought, but susceptible to health problems if given too much water. It's slow growing, but with proper care it can live for decades.

Tip *If you have cats you might consider putting this in a hanging planter, high up out of harm's way – it's not toxic, but can be tempting to chew on.*

Water Drought tolerant. Allow the soil to completely dry out before watering. Check soil every 7–10 days in summer and every 12–14 days in winter

Light Will tolerate low light but would prefer moderate to bright light where it is more likely to produce pups. Position beside a north-facing window, or no further than around 1m (3–4ft) back from an east-, west- or south-facing window

Soil Cacti and succulent soil

Size at maturity Medium to large

Feed Once a month during spring and summer, but dilute to half the suggested strength

Propagate Offsets (the longer the baby plantlets are left to grow on the parent, the better their chances of survival when propagating)

Pets Non-toxic

Prayer plant
Maranta leuconeura

Family Marantaceae

In its native Brazil, the prayer plant grows low and spreads wide in tropical forests. The undersides of the leaves are a striking maroon colour, making it the perfect plant to display in a hanging planter. If growth becomes sparse at the top of the plant, propagate a few cuttings (cut a length of stem that includes a node and at least two or three leaves), and once they have roots, plant them back into the pot to give it a bushier look. See page 57 for more on this plant's incredible ability to lift its leaves at night.

Tip *Thrips and spider mites love this plant; keep your eyes peeled for signs of a problem (see pages 221 and 225).*

Water Would prefer to drink rainwater rather than tap water. Water when approaching dry. Leaves may curl when the plant is thirsty. Check soil every 5–7 days in summer and every 10–12 days in winter

Light They don't like bright light and it can cause their leaves to become faded. Position close to a north-facing window, 1–2m (3–6.5ft) away from an east- or west-facing window, or within 2m (6.5ft) of a south-facing window

Soil General houseplant soil. Would benefit from additions such as perlite, biochar or bark, which improve aeration

Size at maturity Medium

Feed Once or twice a month during spring and summer, but dilute to half the suggested strength

Propagate Stem cutting

Pets Non-toxic

Kentia palm
Howea forsteriana

Family Arecaceae

While the leaves resemble a palm, the stem of a young kentia won't resemble a trunk until the plant is at least 15 to 20 years old, by which point it would be around 12m (40ft) tall. Don't worry about this happening indoors, it's a really slow grower. Native to Lord Howe Island (located between Australia and New Zealand), it is one of the most traded plants in the world, and for good reason: it adds a touch of the tropical to any room and will survive in lower light than many of its counterparts – that's not to say it wouldn't prefer a brighter spot.

Tip *Take care when repotting and only repot if absolutely necessary. The kentia palm has fragile roots and doesn't like them being mishandled, so be very gentle.*

Water Water when the soil is approaching dry. Check soil every 5–7 days in summer and every 12–14 days in winter

Light Although tolerant of low light it can cause it to look a bit leggy, with more stem than fronds. Direct sunlight, especially for a young plant, could lead to sunburn. Position beside a north-facing window or within 2m (6.5ft) of an east-, west- or south-facing window

Soil General houseplant soil, with some sand mixed in for better drainage

Size at maturity Large

Feed Once a month during the growing season (specialist palm feed is available but not essential)

Propagate Division

Pets Non-toxic

Philodendron 'Imperial Green'

Philodendron erubescens
'Imperial Green'

Family Araceae

Philodendrons are native to the tropical rainforests of South America. This one pictured is one I rescued: destined for the bin, it was considered unsuitable for sale because most of its leaves were damaged. Can you imagine this plant being thrown away? I have it sitting close to a north-facing window, and with its large, deep green leaves that are abundant in chlorophyll, it's adept at harnessing light. It throws out gorgeous, glossy leaves regardless of the time of year. The only downside to these beautiful leaves is they act as very good dust collectors – use a moist cloth to clean them at least once a month.

Tip *Creating big leaves takes a lot of energy so keep your philodendron well fed.*

Water Allow the soil to dry out before watering. Check soil every 7–10 days in summer and every 12–14 days in winter

Light Will be happy in most light conditions apart from deep shade and bright direct light. Position close to a north-facing window or within 2m (6.5ft) of an east-, west- or south-facing window

Soil Chunky and airy while also being moisture retentive. An example of this could be a potting mix that contains decomposed green matter and milled bark, with the addition of worm castings, chunky bark and vermiculite

Size at maturity Large

Feed Twice a month while growing (which can be throughout the year). Dilute to half the strength during autumn and winter if it continues to produce leaves

Propagate Stem cutting

Pets Toxic

Purple spiderwort
Tradescantia pallida 'Purpurea'

Family Commelinaceae

In low light, this 'Purpurea' (or 'Purple Heart') will grow, but its leaves will turn dark green instead of the vibrant purple that gives the plant its name. It looks particularly nice in a hanging planter or on a shelf where it can trail downwards. Older plants can get a bit straggly and benefit from being cut back – you can be harsh! Propagate the cuttings in water or soil and plant them back into the pot for a bushier look, or give them to friends. Native to Mexico, where it's considered an invasive species, it forms a dense mat that covers the ground and prevents other species from growing.

Tip *These plants can drink! Because of this, I find the soil can quickly become compacted. Aerate every other time you water by using a chopstick to create channels in the soil.*

Water Thirsty, but also tolerant of drought. Water when the soil is approaching dry. Check soil every 5–7 days in summer and every 10–12 days in winter

Light Will tolerate all light levels but will turn the most spectacular deep purple in brighter light. Will flower if given a few hours of bright indirect sunlight. Will grow beside a north-facing window, or for the best colour place beside an east- or west-facing window or within around 1m (3–4ft) of a south-facing window

Soil General houseplant soil

Size at maturity Medium

Feed Once or twice a month during spring and summer. You may find it grows all year round, in which case feed a few times during autumn and winter but dilute to half the suggested strength

Propagate Stem cutting

Pets Toxic

ZZ plant
Zamioculcas zamiifolia

Family Araceae

I recommend trying to find the black cultivar of the ZZ plant, known as 'Raven'. New growth is particularly striking due to its lime green appearance, which makes a dramatic contrast to the almost black mature leaves. Native to southeastern Africa, the ZZ plant's leaves grow from underground stems called rhizomes, which grow horizontally. This is where the plant stores nutrients, carbohydrates and proteins and the rhizomes can be divided to propagate new plants. Compared to many plants, the ZZ has an unusually high water content and each leaf can last for six months or more, this may be one of the reasons it can survive in low light for weeks without water.

Tip Be patient, your ZZ may not grow for a while and then all of a sudden it will put out a few big new stems. It grows sporadically rather than regularly.

Water Drought tolerant. Allow the soil to completely dry out before watering. Check soil every 7–10 days in summer and every 12–14 days in winter

Light ZZ plants are accepting of all levels of light. May flower if positioned in bright light. Position within 1m (3–4ft) of a north-facing window or within 2m (6.5ft) of an east-, west- or south-facing window

Soil General houseplant soil

Size at maturity Medium

Feed Once a month during spring and summer, but dilute to half the suggested strength

Propagate Division, whole leaf cutting or stem cutting

Pets Toxic

Heartleaf philodendron
Philodendron hederaceum

Family Araceae

This philodendron (native to Central and South America) is a hemiepiphyte, which means it spends part of its life as an epiphyte living on trees. Their seeds germinate in the canopy and initially grow on trees before their roots grow downward, eventually making contact with the ground. I grow my heartleaf philodendron in a self-watering hanging planter where it trails from the ceiling to the floor. In low light the leaves tend to be smaller and spaced far apart on the stem. Trim the stem to promote bushier growth higher up the plant.

Tip *If you ever see your heartleaf philodendron curling its leaves inwards it means it's thirsty. Give it some water and within 24 hours the leaves should open out again.*

Water Allow to dry out between watering. Check soil every 5–7 days in summer and every 10–12 days in winter

Light Tolerant of low light, but might become straggly. For larger leaves, grow in moderate to bright indirect light – it won't tolerate direct bright light. Position close to a north-facing window or within 2m (6.5ft) of an east-, west- or south-facing window

Soil General houseplant soil. Optional addition of a medium that improves aeration

Size at maturity Medium

Feed Once a month, but dilute to half the suggested strength

Propagate Stem cutting

Pets Toxic

Snake plant

Dracaena trifasciata

Family Asparagaceae

The mascot of the low light crew, the snake plant has forever been condemned to a life in the dark, which is a shame because given brighter conditions it will enjoy life to the full and may even reward you with a flower. A spreading or clumping plant with creeping underground stems called rhizomes, it produces clusters of erect leaves up to 1m (3–4ft) tall. In its native habitats in central and western Africa, it uses the crassulacean acid metabolism (CAM) process to withstand drought (see page 42).

Tip *The rhizomes can sometimes push against the pot, distorting the plastic – take this as a clear signal the plant needs to be potted on.*

Water The snake plant has succulent leaves, so treat it as you would any succulent and only water when the soil is completely dry. Low temperatures combined with low light and excessive moisture in the soil will cause root rot. Check soil every 7–10 days in summer and every 14–21 days in winter

Light Will tolerate being kept in almost any level of light intensity apart from complete darkness. May flower if positioned in bright light. Place within 1m (3–4ft) of a north-facing window or within 2m (6.5ft) of an east-, west- or south-facing window

Soil Cacti and succulent soil

Size at maturity Medium

Feed A light feeder, so feed twice a year, once in spring and again in summer

Propagate Division, whole leaf cutting

Pets Toxic

Devil's ivy
Epipremnum aureum

Family Araceae

It's fascinating to me that what constitutes a houseplant in some countries, is considered an invasive weed in others. Devil's ivy is exactly this in Hawaii and Sri Lanka, where it climbs as high as the trees and takes up residence in inhospitable places such as dump sites and along roadsides. However, in our UK homes we can't get enough of them and it's not hard to see why: they will tolerate growing in even the darkest spot, suffer neglect without complaint, look great trailing down from a shelf and are super easy to propagate: just push cuttings back into the soil to make a bushier plant.

Tip *If positioned in bright light, the leaves will become bigger and, if you have a variegated variety, they will produce better variegation.*

Water Allow the soil to completely dry out before watering. Check soil every 7–10 days in summer and every 12–14 days in winter

Light Will grow in almost any light condition including deep shade. Won't tolerate bright direct light, which can cause the leaves to fade and burn. For best results position within 1m (3–4ft) of a north-facing window or within 2m (6.5ft) of an east-, west- or south-facing window

Soil General houseplant soil

Size at maturity Medium

Feed Once or twice a month during spring and summer. It may grow year-round, in which case feed a few times in autumn and winter, but dilute to half the suggested strength

Propagate Stem cutting

Pets Toxic

Arrowhead plant 'Trileaf Wonder'
Syngonium podophyllum
'Trileaf Wonder'

Family Araceae

Arrowhead plants grow in moist and shady conditions in tropical areas of Central and South America. Vigorous, vining plants, they start life on the forest floor, before rapidly advancing up trees to reach the sunlight higher up in the canopy. The 'Trileaf Wonder' has beautiful and unusual shaped leaves that set it apart from more familiar arrowhead plants. Train it up a trellis or moss pole, or let it tumble downwards from a shelf.

Tip *If the vines get too long or straggly, prune the plant and then propagate the cuttings.*

Water Water when approaching dry. Check soil every 5–7 days in summer and every 10–12 days in winter

Light Will tolerate low light, moderate and bright indirect light. Position close to a north-facing window or within 2m (6.5ft) of an east-, west- or south-facing window

Soil General houseplant soil. Optional addition of a medium that improves aeration

Size at maturity Medium

Feed Once a month in spring and summer, but dilute to half the suggested strength

Propagate Stem cutting

Pets Toxic

Peace lily
Spathiphyllum wallisii

Family Araceae

The misleadingly named peace lily is not actually a member of the lily family. Its common name is said to come from the white flower (inflorescence), which symbolises a white flag that's commonly understood as a signal of ceasefire. The inflorescence of the peace lily consists of a leaf-like hood called a 'spathe' within which is enclosed a tube-like structure called a 'spadix'. It is native to the tropical forests of Colombia and Venezuela where it can be found growing on the forest floor or sometimes on rocks in streams.

Tip *The peace lily is good at letting you know when you've left it too long between waterings: the leaves will sag and even flop right down over the pot. It may forgive you doing this once or twice, but let it dry out for too long and it may not recover.*

Water Tap water is fine, but once in a while the soil will benefit from being flushed through with rainwater. Water when the soil is approaching dry. Check every 5–7 days in summer and every 10–12 days in winter

Light Tolerant of low light, but more likely to flower in bright indirect sunlight. Position within 1m (3–4ft) of a north-facing window or within 2m (6.5ft) of an east-, west- or south-facing window. Doesn't like direct sunlight

Soil General houseplant soil

Size at maturity Medium

Feed Not heavy feeders, so feed just once or twice during spring and summer, but dilute to half the suggested strength

Propagate Division, offsets

Pets Not a member of the lily family, but still mildly toxic

Velvet leaf philodendron
Philodendron micans

Family Araceae

If I could have only one plant from this list it would have to be this one. The leaves are among my favourites for their colour, shape and velvety texture. Native to Mexico, where it grows in tropical forests, this plant looks best trailing or hanging in front of a window. In its natural habitat, the vining stems can reach up to 6m (20ft) long, indoors you can expect 1–2m (3–6.5ft). It's in the low-light category, but to appreciate its true nature it needs to be in a spot that receives a few hours of bright indirect light each day.

Tip *If it becomes leggy, trim the stems (include at least one or two nodes) and push the cuttings back into the soil.*

Water Water when soil is approaching dry. Check soil every 5–7 days in summer and every 10–12 days in winter

Light Tolerant of low light, but leaves may be small and spaced far apart on the stem. For best results position beside a north-facing window or within 1m (3–4ft) of an east-, west- or south-facing window

Soil Choose a chunky and airy soil that's also moisture retentive. An example of this could be general houseplant soil with the addition of worm castings, chunky bark and vermiculite

Size at maturity Medium

Feed Once or twice a month during spring and summer. It may grow year-round, in which case feed a few times in autumn and winter, but dilute to half the suggested strength

Propagate Stem cutting

Pets Toxic

Dumb cane
Dieffenbachia seguine

Family Araceae

Native to the tropical Americas, this houseplant has been popular in the UK since the Victorian era, enjoyed for its patterned, paddle-like leaves. Don't worry if one or two of the lower leaves occasionally turn yellow and die, this is a natural part of the life-cycle of a dumb cane. Its sap contains raphides (calcium oxalate crystals) and is toxic if ingested, so this is not a plant to grow if you have curious pets or small children.

Tip *May need to be supported with a cane as it grows taller.*

Water Allow soil to completely dry out before watering. Tolerant of occasional drought. Check soil every 5–7 days in summer and every 12–14 days in winter

Light Tolerant of low light but not deep shade. Will be less prone to health issues in moderate to bright indirect light. Position beside a north-facing window or within around 1–2m (3ft–6.5ft) of an east-, west- or south-facing window

Soil General houseplant soil

Size at maturity Large

Feed Once or twice a month while growing (which can be throughout the year). Dilute to half the suggested strength during autumn and winter if it's still producing leaves

Propagate Stem cutting

Pets Toxic

Moderate Light

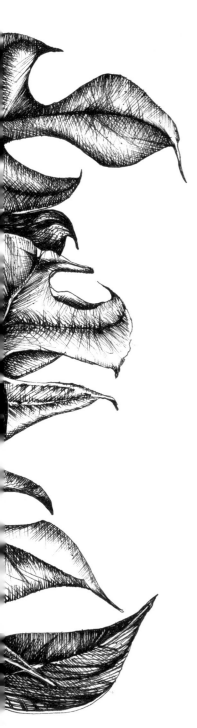

There are few areas on Earth where the sun beats down unobscured for the entire day. Trees, vegetation, hills and buildings cast shadows and create growing environments that are partially shaded or shaded for part of the day. Plants may receive a few hours of direct sunlight in the morning or the afternoon, while being cast into the shade for the rest of the day, or they may be in dappled sunlight filtered through the leaves and branches of overhead trees.

Indoors, moderate light is most likely to be found next to an east- or west-facing window (see page 47). The direction these windows face means that the sun's rays could directly reach the plant for part of the day. Plants positioned around 1–1.5m (3–5ft) away from an unobstructed, south-facing window could also be considered to be receiving moderate, indirect light. The majority of houseplants will grow well in these locations, including ferns, but here are a few of my favourites.

String of hearts
Ceropegia woodii

Family Apocynaceae

This beautiful trailing vine can grow around 2–4m (6–13ft long) and is a succulent native to the southern reaches of Africa. Its small round tubers are used for water and food storage. It also puts out little trumpet-shaped flowers, which although not carnivorous, are able to trap flies for pollination purposes. It can do well outdoors in a hanging basket over summer, but requires some shade. If the top of the vines (those closest to the pot) lose their leaves, propagate a few cuttings and plant them back into the pot.

Tip *Plant in a terracotta pot, as this helps to wick away excess moisture.*

Water Allow the soil to completely dry out between watering. Check soil every 7–10 days in summer and every 12–14 days in winter. Will tolerate periods of drought

Light Choose a spot beside a window that gets at least a few hours of bright indirect sunlight. Pale leaves are usually an indication that it's not receiving adequate light. Position within 60cm (2ft) of an east- or west-facing window or within around 1m (3–4ft) of a south-facing window

Soil Cacti and succulent soil

Size at maturity Small to medium

Feed Once or twice during the growing season, but dilute to half the suggested strength

Propagate Stem cutting, tuber

Pets Non-toxic

Staghorn fern
Platycerium bifurcatum

Family Polypodiaceae

The staghorn fern produces two types of fronds: basal (shield-shaped) and fertile (antler-shaped). In its native eastern Australia, the staghorn fern is attached to trees, and the basal fronds act as protection for the roots and also help to gather nutrients and moisture. These fronds look like a shield or a plate and they naturally turn brown before the plant regrows another. Don't be tempted to cut these off as it can damage the plant's ability to take up nutrients.

Tip *These ferns can be mounted on a board and hung on the wall, but be aware that warm air rises and so the potting medium will dry out more quickly. It's also not easy or convenient to water a plant on a board. Mine lives in a pot on a low shelf, next to a northeast-facing window and has been thriving for years.*

Water Frequency will depend on whether the plant is mounted on a board or in a pot. It's likely that you will need to check on the moisture level twice a week during the spring and summer months if it's mounted on a board, and once a week if it's in a pot. In both cases, allow the soil to approach dry before watering

Light Moderate light, with a few hours of bright light. Position within 60cm (2ft) of an east- or west-facing window or within 1m (3–4ft) of a south-facing window

Soil Use a potting mix that contains 50% chunky bark, such as a half-and-half mix of general houseplant soil and chunky orchid bark

Size at maturity Medium

Feed Once or twice during the growing season, but dilute to half the suggested strength

Propagate Division

Pets Non-toxic

Forest cactus
Pfeiffera boliviana

Family Cactaceae

Epiphytic cacti, such as this forest cactus, can be found growing on tree branches in the tropical jungles of South America (this one is native to Bolivia). The thin, flat stems resemble leaves and they can be easily propagated: cut off a section of any length and simply plant the cut end into very lightly moistened soil. Fill a pot with cuttings to make a full plant.

Tip *If you see brown areas, check for mealybugs, which love to feast on this plant (see page 223).*

Water Allow soil to completely dry out before watering. Will tolerate short periods of drought. Check soil every 5–7 days in summer and every 10–14 days in winter

Light Hang within 60cm (2ft) of an east- or west-facing window or within around 1m (3–4ft) of a south-facing window

Soil Cacti and succulent soil mixed with a handful of general houseplant soil

Size at maturity Medium

Feed Once or twice during the growing season

Propagate Stem cutting

Pets Toxic

Rabbit's foot fern
Davallia fejeensis

Family Polypodiaceae

Why this wasn't nicknamed the 'tarantula fern' I will never understand. I am terrified of spiders (something I am very ashamed to say as a nature lover), but despite the rhizomes bearing a strong resemblance to hairy tarantula legs, I absolutely adore this plant. It's not your typical fern – it won't turn brown and wilt the minute the soil dries out – and propagating it is something you must try (see page 240).

Tip *While most rhizomes are underground energy stores, this fern likes to keep its rhizomes above ground. Allow them to creep across the soil and over the edge of the pot and don't be tempted to bury them as they will rot.*

Water Will tolerate short periods of drought. Water when approaching dry. You can mist the rhizomes as they absorb water. Check soil every 5–7 days in summer and every 10–12 days in winter

Light Moderate, with a few hours of bright light (mine hangs beneath a skylight). Position beside or within 60cm (2ft) of an east- or west-facing window, or within around 1m (3–4ft) of a south-facing window

Soil General houseplant soil with a medium that improves aeration, such as bark and grit. This plant has a shallow root system, so the pot doesn't need be too deep

Size at maturity Medium

Feed Once or twice during the growing season, but dilute to half the suggested strength

Propagate Rhizome

Pets Non-toxic

Chinese money plant / Pancake plant
Pilea peperomioides

A much loved member of the nettle family, the Chinese money plant is a semi-succulent native to central China, with distinctive circular leaves that can reach over 15cm (6in) in diameter. Given good exposure to light, it is fast growing and can double in size in a year, producing numerous offspring that can be gifted to friends and family; when the babies reach a third of the size of the parent plant, they can easily be propagated (see page 238).

Tip *A plant which has become leggy or has rotting roots can be saved: chop off the main stem and propagate it in water or soil.*

Water Allow the soil to dry out between watering. Being semi-succulent means it will tolerate short periods of drought. Check soil every 5–7 days in summer and every 12–14 days in winter

Light Moderate, with a few hours of bright direct light. Position beside or within 60cm (2ft) of an east- or west-facing window or within around 1m (3–4ft) of a south-facing window

Soil General houseplant soil, with the addition of a medium that improves aeration

Size at maturity Medium

Feed Once a month during the growing season, but dilute to half the suggested strength

Propagate Offsets

Pets Non-toxic

Delta maidenhair fern

Adiantum raddianum

Family Pteridaceae

The Delta maidenhair fern is native to Mexico and tropical regions of America where it can be found growing on forest floors and in rocky crevices, walls, river banks and coastal cliffs. Ferns are often positioned in the dark, deeply shaded areas of our homes; we have been led to believe that because many of them thrive on the forest floor, we should find them a low-light spot in our homes. It's simply not the case and few will survive in areas that are too far from a window.

Tip *Use a self-watering pot to reduce the risk of the soil drying out between watering.*

Water Allow the soil to approach dry (but not completely dry) before watering. This fern is unforgiving of completely dry soil and the fronds will quickly turn brown and die. Misting is not necessary or helpful to the health of the plant. Check soil every 3–4 days in summer and every 7–10 days in winter

Light Despite growing in damp and shady places, it won't tolerate deep shade so place it somewhere that receives moderate to bright light, or even direct sunlight, for a few hours a day. Position within 60cm (2ft) of an east- or west-facing window or within 60–90cm (2–3ft) of a south-facing window

Soil General houseplant soil

Size at maturity Small to medium

Feed Once or twice during the growing season

Propagate Division

Pets Non-toxic

Swiss cheese plant
Monstera deliciosa

Family Araceae

What can I say about the ubiquitous monstera that hasn't already been said a thousand times? They are beloved for their ease of care, their ability to survive in less than ideal light conditions and their good looks. Their large, fenestrated leaves are the subject of much research and debate, as it's not totally clear why they have holes and gaps, though one of the theories is that it may help with water uptake. In their native Mexico and Central America, they live in the understorey of forests where water is harder to come by – the holes may allow for rainfall to pass through the leaves and down to the ground below, where it can be more easily reached.

Tip *If the aerial roots (used by the plant for support and to search for sustenance) become too unruly, tuck them back into the soil.*

Water Water when soil is approaching dry. Check soil every 5–7 days in summer and every 10–14 days in winter

Light Monsteras are often positioned in low light, where they're more likely to succumb to health issues. For a happy plant, place within 60cm (2ft) of an east- or west-facing window, next to a north-facing window, or 1–2m (3-6.5ft) back from a south-facing window

Soil General houseplant soil with the addition of a few handfuls of a medium that improves aeration

Size at maturity Large

Feed Twice a month during the growing season

Propagate Stem cutting

Pets Toxic

Moth orchid / Moon orchid
Phalaenopsis amabilis

Family Orchidaceae

Moth orchids can flower for three months, sometimes longer, and at almost any time of year. After flowering they require a period of rest, but will bloom again with some basic care (see page 209). Epiphytic orchids, such as this one, have air roots that absorb moisture and nutrients from the air and from the bark of trees. They should only be grown in an orchid potting mix, which usually consists of bark and helps this plant recreate the way it absorbs moisture in its native habitats, which include Malaysia and the Philippines.

Tip *If you see green roots, don't water; if you see silver roots, it's time to water.*

Water Allow the potting mix to completely dry out before soaking (see page 65 for more on watering orchids)

Light Position on a north-facing windowsill, within 60cm (2ft) of an east- or west-facing window, or around 1m (3–4ft) back from a south-facing window. In summer, take care not to allow the leaves to get scorched and move them off the windowsill if in direct sunlight

Soil Orchid bark

Size at maturity Small

Feed Add orchid feed to the water once a month when soaking the plant

Propagate Occasionally, a baby plant can grow from the stem (called a 'keiki'). Wait for the keiki to grow at least several roots before detaching it and potting it into orchid bark

Pets Non-toxic

Rhaphidophora
Rhaphidophora tetrasperma

Family Araceae

With leaf fenestrations that look similar to those of the Swiss cheese plant (see page 133), this plant (native to Thailand and Malaysia) is often incorrectly named a mini monstera or monstera minima. The *Rhaphidophora tetrasperma* looks just as attractive as a monstera and can be grown up a support or allowed to vine downwards from a hanging planter. They are fast growers (given the correct light) and can be easily propagated, so don't be afraid to give very long stems a hard prune and make lots more plants from the cuttings. Check regularly for signs of pests as thrips adore this plant (see page 225).

Tip *If your plant isn't receiving enough light, the leaves will grow small and far apart on the stem.*

Water Allow soil to completely dry out in between watering. Check soil every 5–7 days in summer and every 10–14 days in winter

Light Tolerant of a variety of light conditions, but will do best positioned within 60cm (2ft) of a window facing west or east and within around 1m (3–4ft) of a south-facing window. Make sure the leaves aren't so close that they get burnt by direct sunlight

Soil General houseplant soil, with the addition of a few handfuls of a medium to make it more free-draining

Size at maturity Medium to large

Feed Once a month in the growing season

Propagate Stem cutting

Pets Toxic

Emerald feather fern
Asparagus densiflorus
Sprengeri Group

Family Asparagaceae

As ferns go, this one is pretty resilient. Tolerant of less-than-perfect care, this wild, feathery fern will forgive the occasional dry spell, but will alert you if it goes on for too long with leaves that turn brown and drop to the floor. If this happens, cut back the dead stem or stems and wait for regrowth. Native to southern Africa, this sprawling fern can reach around 1m (3–4ft) in both width and length. It looks particularly good suspended from the ceiling in a hanging planter.

Tip *Watch out for the thorns along the stems as they can scratch.*

Water Allow soil to approach dry before watering. Check soil every 3–4 days in summer and every 7–10 days in winter

Light Place beside a north-facing window or 30–60cm (1–2ft) back from an east- or west-facing window, or around 1m (3–4ft) back from a south-facing window

Soil General houseplant soil

Size at maturity Medium

Feed Use a general houseplant feed once a month in spring and summer, or top dress with worm castings once or twice during the growing season

Propagate Division

Pets Toxic

Angel wings
Caladium

Family Araceae

Caladiums can be grown indoors or planted outside in the warmer months. Their spectacular leaves come in a variety of colours, some with speckles or veins in contrasting colours, and each leaf can grow as large as 50cm (20in) long – I imagine that's a common sight in their native habitats in Central and South America. The foliage will die back in autumn as the plant goes into dormancy, and you can store the tubers over winter and pot them again the following year (see page 180).

Tip *The foliage will grow towards the source of light; turn the pot a little every few days to avoid the leaves all facing the same direction.*

Water Allow the soil to approach dry before watering. Check it every 3–4 days in summer

Light Position on a north-facing windowsill, within 60cm (2ft) of an east- or west-facing window, or within 60–90cm (2–3ft) of a south-facing window. Direct sunlight may scorch the leaves

Soil General houseplant soil. You can make an optional addition of vermiculite to help retain moisture while also improving aeration

Size at maturity Small to medium

Feed Once or twice a month

Propagate Division

Pets Toxic

Fishbone prayer plant / Never never plant
Ctenanthe burle-marxii

Family Marantaceae

A close relation to the genera *Calathea* and *Maranta*, this Brazilian native is also in the *Marantaceae* family and shares the common characteristic of nyctinastic movement (see page 57). We are led to believe that this plant will suffer without high humidity, which isn't necessarily the case. Misting can contribute to fungal leaf infections and pebble trays do very little to help with increasing humidity. Mine does just fine living in the normal levels of humidity in my home. Problems are more likely to be due to a lack of light combined with too much water.

Tip *Spider mites and thrips find these plants irresistible; check them regularly for any signs of an infestation (see pages 221 and 225).*

Water Leaves will potentially twist and curl when thirsty. Water when approaching dry. If possible, flush the soil with rainwater once in a while to avoid a build-up of salts. Check soil every 5–7 days in summer and every 7–10 days in winter

Light Doesn't like direct sunlight on its leaves, so don't put it right beside the window. Opt for a position at least 30–60cm (1–2ft) back, and perhaps a little more if the window faces south. If the position is too bright, the foliage may become faded

Soil General houseplant soil

Size at maturity Small to medium

Feed Once a month during the growing season, but dilute to half the suggested strength to avoid a build-up of excess minerals in the soil

Propagate Division

Pets Non-toxic

Whale fin

Dracaena masoniana

Family Asparagaceae

This plant's common name refers to the appearance of the leaf, which protrudes from the soil like a giant fin. In its native habitat in central parts of Africa, this plant grows dozens of leaves, but indoors, with a pot constricting its growth, it is generally slow growing and you may only get four or five leaves over the course of a few years. It's common for whale fins to have small nicks or scars on their leaves – you can see mine has a split at the top – and this does not affect their health in any way.

Tip *The subtle patternation and colours of the leaf can be brought out by positioning the plant in bright indirect light.*

Water Allow the soil to completely dry out between watering. Check soil every 7–10 days in summer and once a month in winter

Light Position beside a north-facing window, within 60cm (2ft) of an east- or west-facing window, or around 1m (3–4ft) from a south-facing window

Soil Cacti and succulent soil

Size at maturity Medium

Feed Whale fins are light feeders – feed once or twice during the growing season, but dilute to half the suggested strength

Propagate Division, leaf cutting

Pets Toxic

Norfolk Island pine
Araucaria heterophylla

Family Araucariaceae

I discovered the Norfolk Island pine while looking for a Christmas tree. I don't like the idea of chopping trees down just for Christmas, so I bought one of these instead, which I can keep year round. The pine is named after its native habitat, Norfolk Island, which is a tiny landmass in the southwestern Pacific off the east coast of Australia.

Tip *It will live happily indoors, but I wait until the risk of frost has passed in spring and put it outside in a partially shaded spot until late autumn. Don't forget to feed it.*

Water Allow soil to approach dry before watering

Light Tolerant of moderate to low light but will become a brighter shade of green, and healthier, if given a few hours of direct sunlight in the morning or late afternoon. Position within 60cm (2ft) of an east- or west-facing window or 60–90cm (2–3ft) from a south-facing window

Soil Use all-purpose garden or general houseplant soil and add 25% sand/grit to improve drainage

Size at maturity Medium to large

Feed Feed through spring and summer, twice a month

Propagate Seed

Pets Toxic

Polka dot begonia
Begonia maculata

Family Begoniaceae

Want to make a bit of a statement and can't afford a work of art? Just buy a polka dot begonia instead. This is one bold and dramatic plant – the houseplant equivalent to a peacock. And just when you think the Brazilian native can't get any more beautiful, out pop pale white/pink flowers any time from late winter through to spring. Given proper care it could reach over 1m (3–4ft) in height.

Tip *Turn the pot regularly to prevent it becoming one sided, as the leaves tend to turn to face the sun.*

Water Water when approaching dry. Check once every 3–4 days in summer and once every 7–10 days in winter

Light Position within 60cm (2ft) of an east- or west-facing window or 60–90cm (2–3ft) from a south-facing window. Keep an eye on the leaves and make sure they aren't being scorched by direct sunlight or becoming crispy

Soil General houseplant soil with the addition of a few handfuls of a medium that improves aeration

Size at maturity Medium

Feed Twice a month during the growing season, but dilute to half the suggested strength

Propagate Stem cutting

Pets Toxic

Bright Light

Outdoors, an area receiving bright direct sunlight is considered to be one where the sun beats down for most of the day, unfiltered by other plants or objects. Indoors, direct sunlight coming in through our windows doesn't have the same intensity as it does outdoors, but it can still stress or burn a plant. Bright indirect light doesn't 'directly' reach the plant, so is less intense and less likely to burn a plant. Dramatic changes in colour, such as a plant turning red or bleached, or scorched leaves can be signs that the light is too intense.

Areas in the home that receive bright light are mostly suitable for plants that are adapted to arid environments, such as desert cacti, or those that need a greater intensity of sunlight to thrive. Plants that require bright light would do better outside, but if you live in a climate that makes this impossible, give them the next best thing – position them on an east- or west-facing windowsill or within 0–1m (0–3ft) of a south-facing window (see page 47).

String of pearls
Curio rowleyanus

Family Asteraceae

This beautiful, unusual, cascading succulent resembles rosary beads or a necklace of pearls and is native to the southern tip of Africa. If you're buying a string of pearls from a shop or garden centre, check to see if the soil is very wet. Growers often use the same soil for lots of different houseplants, regardless of their specific requirements, and if the soil is dense and heavy, it could be holding too much moisture, which might already be causing a problem for the roots. It's best to choose one that isn't in damp soil or be prepared to repot it when you get home.

Tip *They have a small, shallow root system; planting one in a pot that's too big can lead to root rot.*

Water Allow the soil to completely dry out before watering. Check soil every 5–7 days in summer and every 10–12 days in winter

Light Bright light, with a few hours of direct sunlight hitting the top of the pot. Hang beside an east- or west-facing window, it will also be happy 30–60cm (1–2ft) back from a south-facing window. Will enjoy being outside in the warm summer months

Soil Cacti and succulent soil, as this plant needs excellent drainage

Size at maturity Small to medium

Feed Be cautious using synthetic fertilisers: dilute to at least half the suggested strength and only feed once or twice a year in spring and summer. Alternatively, use something natural like worm castings and top dress the soil twice a year

Propagate Stem cutting, simple layering

Pets Toxic

Bird of paradise
Strelitzia nicolai

Family Strelitziaceae

Strelitzia nicolai has a white flower, while *S. reginae* has an orange one, but don't expect either species to bloom unless the plant is mature – around three years old and over. In its native southern Africa, the spathe of the flower is used as a perch by sunbirds who steal nectar and unwittingly pollinate the plant. Don't be upset if your bird of paradise develops splits in its leaves, this is completely normal and is thought to be an adaptation to allow wind to pass through. It's a slow grower, so buy big if you can afford it.

Tip *This plant loves warm sun: put it outside in summer for a pick me up. Bring it back in when temperatures drop to lower than 12°C as it's not hardy.*

Water Allow soil to completely dry out before watering. Check soil every 5–7 days in summer and every 10–12 days in winter

Light The only way to keep these plants happy is to give them as much light as possible. There is no point buying one unless there is space for it right beside an east- or west-facing window or 30–60cm (1–2ft) back from a south-facing window. Failure to give this plant bright light will result in disappointment

Soil General houseplant soil. Optional addition of grit to aid drainage

Size at maturity Large

Feed Twice a month during spring and summer or top dress with worm castings three or four times a year

Propagate Division

Pets Toxic

Lithops / Living stones / Pebble plants
Lithops

Family Aizoaceae

Lithops are fascinating plants that have adapted to survive in the deserts of their native southern Africa. These tiny succulents have two leaves, bloated with water, which would make them a very attractive snack for a thirsty animal in the desert. They manage to avoid being eaten by camouflaging themselves as stones and pebbles, so animals simply don't notice them. Living stones survive in climates that receive as little as 10cm (4in) of rain each year.

Tip *After flowering, new leaves will slowly develop from the fissure – don't water while the old leaves are drying out, wait until they have completely shrivelled up.*

Water Withhold water after flowering (if they are mature enough to flower) or from early autumn until the following spring. If you see them shrivelling add a tiny amount of water. Water in mid- to late-spring, allowing the soil to completely dry out between watering. If there is a prolonged period of overcast weather, withhold water until it becomes brighter

Light Bright light is absolutely necessary, with 4–5 hours of direct sunlight needed each day, so place on a south-facing windowsill

Soil Cacti and succulent soil. Add in an extra handful of grit. The majority of the soil should be gritty and sandy, with only a very small percentage of organic matter

Size at maturity Small

Feed Not necessary

Propagate Grow from seed

Pets Non-toxic

Dead plant
Euphorbia platyclada

Family Euphorbiaceae

This is definitely the Marmite of the plant world: to some, this Madagascan native looks like a pot of dead sticks, but to others (including me) it's uniquely beautiful and a favourite member of the *Euphorbia* genus. In bright direct light the mottled pattern of pinks and greens will become more colourful, and if you look closely you might see tiny yellow or green flowers appear at the top of the stems.

Tip *Can be placed outside during the spring and summer months as long as it can be protected from excess rain and wind.*

Water Allow soil to completely dry out before watering. Check soil every 7–10 days in summer and once a month in winter

Light Position within 30cm (1ft) of a south-facing window

Soil Cacti and succulent soil

Size at maturity Small

Feed Once or twice in the growing season, but dilute to half the suggested strength

Propagate Stem cutting from branching point

Pets Toxic

Air plant
Tillandsia

Family Bromeliaceae

Many species of *Tillandsia* can be found growing in full sun on cliffs and high up in the canopies of forests in tropical and subtropical America. Indoors, they should receive as much bright indirect light as possible, which can include a few hours of direct morning or late afternoon sun, but don't let them fry in midday sun in summer. Older leaves may turn brown and die, which is normal, but if lots start crisping up, it could be a sign of dehydration caused by too much direct sun.

Tip *Be creative about how you display your air plants – they can look great placed around the base of another plant; this also serves as a reminder to water them.*

Water If misting, do it as often as you like, if soaking, do this once or twice a week (see page 65)

Light Bright, indirect light with a few hours of direct sunlight. Position beside an east- or west-facing window, or 30–60cm (1–2ft) back from a south-facing window

Soil None

Size at maturity Small

Feed Use a specialist bromeliad or air plant fertiliser once a month

Propagate Offsets. Once an air plant starts to produce pups, the parent will slowly start to decline in health

Pets Non-toxic

Cape sundew

Drosera capensis

Family Droraceae

Buying a few carnivorous sundew plants is a great natural way to help control a fungus gnat infestation (see page 218). The insects are lured in by the sticky sap on the leaf hairs and become stuck, the leaf then slowly rolls onto the prey and begins the process of digestion. Native to the southern tip of Africa, cape sundews will grow all year round indoors as long as they have warm, bright light. In cooler temperatures, they stop growing altogether. They can be planted outside around the margins of a pond, but it's best to cover them or bring them indoors over winter.

Tip *It's a good idea to keep this plant in a self-watering pot so it doesn't dry out. Alternatively, plant into a terracotta pot with a saucer below, then fill the saucer with water and the terracotta will absorb it, keeping the soil moist.*

Water Must be kept moist. Don't let it dry out. Don't use tap water – collect rainwater

Light Position within 30cm (1ft) of a south-facing window

Soil Carnivorous plants are usually grown in a peat-based soil; thankfully, there are now peat-free options available. A quick internet search will bring up the companies specialising in peat-free carnivorous plant substrates

Size at maturity Small

Feed Feed is not necessary as they catch their own, but if they aren't catching anything you might need to step in and drop a few insects on the leaves

Propagate Leaf cuttings, division

Pets Non-toxic

Peanut cactus
Echinopsis chamaecereus

Family Cactaceae

The young stems of this plant bear a resemblance to peanuts, and with age, these lengthen and form clusters that look more like fingers. Positioned in bright light, this Argentine cactus will produce numerous, large scarlet flowers in late spring and early summer. Unfortunately, these blooms are short lived and may last less than a week, opening in the day and closing up at night. Compared to many other cacti, it grows quickly.

Tip *If its buds start to fall off during the flowering season, the plant might not be getting enough water.*

Water Allow soil to completely dry out before watering. Check soil every 7–10 days in summer, withhold water November to March

Light Place on a south-facing windowsill in bright, direct sunlight

Soil Cacti and succulent soil

Size at maturity Small

Feed Once or twice during spring and summer, but dilute to half the suggested strength

Propagate Stem cutting – remove a stem and plant into soil

Pets Non-toxic

Climbing aloe
Aloiampelos ciliaris

Family Asphodelaceae

For those looking for something a little different to the familiar aloe vera, *Aloiampelos ciliaris* (formerly *Aloe ciliaris*) is an unusual climbing aloe. In the wild (it is native to the southern tip of Africa) it reaches 5–10m (16–32ft) tall. As a houseplant, it's unlikely to reach more than around 1.5m (5ft), but with its heavy succulent leaves, it will need support so that it doesn't topple over. It also needs as much light as you can give it.

Tip *Will happily live outside in spring and summer, after the risk of frost has passed.*

Water Allow soil to completely dry out between watering. Check soil once every 7–10 days in summer, and once or twice from November to March

Light Position within 30cm (1ft) of a south-facing window

Soil Cacti and succulent soil

Size at maturity Medium

Feed Once or twice in spring and summer

Propagate Stem cutting, offsets

Pets Toxic

Elephant ear 'Pink Dragon'
Alocasia 'Pink Dragon'

Family Araceae

The tropical elephant ear's striking pink stems and perfect, glossy leaves could, at first glance, look artificial. More forgiving of less-than-perfect care than you might expect, the 'Pink Dragon' is a good choice for those wanting dramatic foliage without the dramatic attitude. I have mine on an east-facing windowsill that is partially obscured by the building next door, but it does get a few hours of direct morning sun in spring and summer.

Tip *Won't appreciate direct midday sun in summer, when the light is at its most intense, as it could cause the leaves to scorch.*

Water Allow the soil to approach dry before watering. Check soil once every 5–7 days in summer and every 12–14 days in winter

Light Bright indirect light, but can handle some direct sun in the morning or late afternoon. Position beside an east- or west-facing window, or 30–60cm (1–2ft) back from a south-facing window

Soil General houseplant soil with a handful of a medium to improve drainage

Size at maturity Medium

Feed Once or twice a month in spring and summer

Propagate Division

Pets Toxic

False shamrock
Oxalis triangularis

Family Oxalidaceae

Commonly known as false shamrock because of its three leaflets and clover-like appearance, this beautiful plant is native to tropical South America where it creeps along the ground and grows from tubers. The leaflets show nyctinastic movement (see page 57), opening in light and closing in darkness; they may also close if the light is too bright. Towards the end of the growing season the plant will begin to look droopy and dishevelled, a sure sign that it is going into dormancy. Stop watering, let the plant die back naturally and then cut off the dead leaves (see page 180). The period of dormancy may last anywhere from weeks to months. As soon as you see new shoots emerging, place the pot back in a bright spot and slowly resume watering.

Tip *Don't panic if the plant collapses, it is most likely to be thirsty and can be revived with a good soak of water.*

Water Allow the soil to approach dry before watering. Don't wait for it to wilt before watering. Check soil once every 4–7 days in spring and summer

Light Bright indirect light. Place on an east- or west-facing windowsill or 60-90cm (2–3ft) back from a south-facing window

Soil General houseplant soil

Size at maturity Small to medium

Feed Once or twice a month, but dilute to half the suggested strength

Propagate Division

Pets Toxic

Monkey tail cactus
Cleistocactus colademononis

Family Cactaceae

I love the monkey tail cactus! I get that its unusual appearance isn't for everyone, but that's exactly what I love about it. It's weird, it's dramatic, it looks like a hairy octopus and it demands very little in terms of care. I would love to see one in its natural habitat, growing on rock faces that protrude above the tropical jungles of Bolivia. The 'tails', which initially begin upright, go on to grow downwards and can reach an amazing 2.5m (8ft) long (although this would be rare for an indoor plant) and they can produce beautiful red flowers. They love being outside during the warmer summer months, ideally suspended from a tree in a semi-shaded spot.

Tip *If a piece breaks off, just push it gently back into the soil and it will take root. It may also grow an offset from the broken area giving you more plants.*

Water Allow soil to completely dry out in between watering. Check soil every 7–10 days in summer and every 10–14 days in winter

Light Position hanging beside an east- or west-facing window, or 60–90cm (2–3ft) back from a south-facing window. Can tolerate a few hours of direct sun in the morning or late afternoon

Soil Cacti and succulent soil

Size at maturity Medium

Feed Once or twice during the growing season

Propagate Stem cutting, offset

Pets Toxic

Jade plant / Money tree

Crassula ovata

Family Crassulaceae

The tortoise of the succulent world, *Crassula ovata* is a slow-growing species native to southern Africa and it can live for decades. As it matures, this plant's stem begins to resemble a trunk and the overall shape of the plant becomes like that of a small tree. Given plenty of bright light it may reward you with beautiful white or pinkish flowers. Mature jade plants can be expensive, so if you want a large one without the wait, check out your local Gumtree, Facebook Marketplace or similar, where it may be possible to pick one up at a fraction of the price.

Tip *When stressed by too much sunlight and a lack of water, its leaves become thin instead of plump, and they turn purple/red.*

Water Allow soil to completely dry out between watering. Check soil once every 7–10 days in summer and once or twice between November and March

Light Bright indirect sunlight with a few hours of direct sun in the morning or late afternoon. Place on an east- or west-facing windowsill or 30–60cm (1–2ft) back from a south-facing window

Soil Cacti and succulent soil

Size at maturity Medium

Feed Once or twice in spring and summer, but dilute to half the suggested strength

Propagate Leaf or stem cutting

Pets Toxic

Ghost cactus / Candelabra tree
Euphorbia ingens 'Variegata'

Family Euphorbiaceae

This characterful plant, native to regions across southern and eastern Africa, is not actually a cactus, but rather a member of the *Euphorbia* genus, commonly referred to as spurge. The sap from this group of plants has been used in purgative medicines throughout history. The word 'spurge' comes from the French word *espurgier*, which means 'to purge'. It goes without saying that the sap of this plant is toxic to both humans and pets. The ghostly colour is enhanced if you keep it in bright sunlight or underneath a grow light.

Tip *Rotate the pot regularly so that the plant doesn't begin to lean towards the window as it reaches for light.*

Water Allow the soil to completely dry out between watering. Check soil every 10–12 days in summer, withhold water from November to March

Light Bright light, with direct sunlight in the morning or late afternoon. Position beside an east- or west-facing window. Will also be happy within 30cm (1ft) of a south-facing window

Soil Cacti and succulent soil

Size at maturity Large

Feed Use a feed that's low in nitrogen two or three times during the growing season. If using an all-purpose feed, dilute to half the suggested strength

Propagate Stem cutting from branching point

Pets Toxic

Fiddle leaf fig
Ficus lyrata

Family Moraceae

All too often I see fiddle leaf figs in shops and homes covered in a layer of dust, far away from a source of light, with just a few droopy leaves hanging off a tall trunk. These plants are native to western Africa and need ample bright light to do well. They will express their unhappiness with their environment by dropping their leaves, and this could be brought on by cold temperatures, low light, an issue with watering or a draught. I don't mean to make this sound like a difficult plant to please, rather I'm stressing the importance of getting the positioning of it just right... and then leaving it there.

Tip *Start with a compact* Ficus lyrata *'Bambino' to get used to their care needs before investing in a tree.*

Water Allow the soil to approach dry before watering. Check soil every 5–7 days in summer and every 14–21 days in winter

Light Bright indirect light, with a few hours of direct morning or afternoon sun. Place beside an east- or west-facing window, or 60–90cm (2–3ft) back from a south-facing window

Soil General houseplant soil. Optional addition of fine milled bark and biochar to improve aeration

Size at maturity Large

Feed Enjoys a good feed once or twice a month in the spring and summer

Propagate Don't bother trying to propagate a leaf that falls off, it may grow roots but it's very unlikely to turn into a full plant. Stem cutting is the best bet

Pets Toxic

Fan palm / Footstool palm
Saribus rotundifolius

Family Arecaceae

This compact, slow-growing palm (native to swampland and rainforest areas in and around Borneo, New Guinea and the Philippines) is perfect for small homes. Despite its size, it makes a dramatic statement with its circular, fan-shaped leaves. Watch out for the spines along the stem. Be warned, this palm won't forgive you for letting the soil completely dry out and will quickly wilt. No amount of water will make it recover once this has happened.

Tip *It will occasionally need its leaves cleaned – use a damp cloth to keep them dust free.*

Water Allow the soil to approach dry before watering. Check soil once every 3–5 days in summer and every 7–10 days in winter

Light Position beside an east- or west-facing window, or 30–60cm (1–2ft) back from a south-facing window. It will enjoy a few hours of direct sunlight in the morning or afternoon

Soil General houseplant soil with the optional addition of 25% sand/grit for improved drainage

Size at maturity Medium

Feed Once a month during the growing season, but dilute to half the suggested strength

Propagate Seed

Pets Non-toxic

Rescue & Propagate

Rescuing Plants

Usually, I'd be very excited about the prospect of being able to buy houseplants within walking distance of my house, but I couldn't have been less excited when a local hardware store decided to branch out into selling plants. The shop in question wasn't designed with plants in mind and has very little natural light. Predictably, within a week or two of the plants arriving on the shelves, it resembled a crime scene, with more of them dead than alive. The culprit was clear: a lack of light.

Rescuing plants, whether they are your own or from a shop, is like playing a game of Cluedo – or rather, Plant Cluedo. You must assess the evidence in order to work out the 'who, what and where' involved in causing the plant to become unhappy. In Plant Cluedo we're not looking for a specific person to blame for the murder of a plant – this is not about naming and shaming – the purpose of this game is to become a detective and dig down into the evidence to build a strong case for what is causing the plant to look unwell. Like a doctor diagnosing a patient, identifying the cause of the symptoms is the only way you can hope to rescue a plant.

On my mission to save neglected plants, playing Plant Cluedo has become second nature. Once you understand the basic requirements of a plant it becomes obvious which weapons have been used to cause harm.

Who — Establish the species of plant and find out about its natural habitat. This will give you vital information that can help you determine why its current environment might be making it unhappy.

What — Find out what weapon has been used to cause harm to the plant. The elements needed for a plant to survive – light, water, warmth and so on – need to be considered. In addition, evidence of pests could point to potential suspects.

Where — Look at where your plant is placed; the environment will have a huge impact on its survival.

Diagnosing what's wrong with an unhealthy plant isn't always a simple task, there are many aspects of the care and the environment that need to be taken into consideration, as well as the appearance of the plant itself. I often get sent photos of ailing plants, along with a brief message: 'Please help! What's wrong with my plant?'. What I'm being shown are the symptoms, but what I can't always see is the cause: how much light the plant is getting, how much water it is receiving, what type of soil it is planted in, whether it is near an air-conditioning unit, in a draught or by a radiator. Without these vital pieces of evidence, I can't build a case file. Would a detective arrest a suspect based purely on a photo of the crime scene?

Jumping to conclusions without looking for the evidence is not going to help revive a sick plant and can often be the final nail in the coffin. Give a wilted plant water because you think it looks thirsty and you may be finishing off a plant that is already drowning.

Deciding what a plant needs based purely on how it looks is a common mistake and the most easily avoided. Before reaching for the watering can, look at all the evidence, build a case file, and then go on to make an informed decision on what the course of action should be.

Symptoms, Diagnosis and Solutions

Plant responses to functional disorders are referred to as 'symptoms' and are primarily caused by issues with water, light, nutrient deficiencies, temperature, pathogens, humidity or pests. The symptoms and causes outlined in the following pages are based on the most common problems houseplant growers experience.

When it's time to say goodbye

Rescuing plants isn't always possible, some will not make it through the stress they have already suffered. Just because my suggestions have worked for some plants does not mean they will work for all. A plant in poor health is stressed and weakened – some of my suggestions are going to temporarily add more stress, and only time will tell if the plant can make a full recovery.

As with a patient, you need to check for vital signs before declaring a plant dead. If none of these can be found, I'm afraid the plant will not recover.

Growth Has the plant stopped growing (i.e. there are no new leaves)?

Colour Is the whole plant brown or yellow, including all the leaves and the stem?

Roots Are the roots mushy or brittle and easily snapped off?

If you can answer 'yes' to all the above, the plant is dead and will not survive. Facing up to the fact that, despite our best efforts and our love, a plant is not going to pull through is hard, but important lessons have (hopefully) been learnt. The next plant you buy owes its life to the one that died before it and the same mistakes won't be made again. But if you can answer 'no' to any of the questions, then there is still hope for saving it or propagating a piece of the plant (see page 228).

If it's a pest that is impacting your plant, you have my sympathy. Battling an infestation can be disheartening if nothing seems to be working, but I have successfully managed to eradicate scale and thrips by cutting a plant right back to the base. Most pests need the leaves to feed on, if the leaves are removed, so is their source of food, so chop the plant back to near the base before giving up. If the infestation is really bad, you have nothing to lose by trying. If the pests come back after cutting down the plant, then I respect your decision to give up and throw it away. Sometimes the fight just isn't worth the stress and hassle – or the risk of the pests infesting your entire collection. Trying everything before giving up will allow you to buy another plant with a clear conscience.

Yellow Leaves

**Too much water/
lack of light**

**Chlorosis is a term used to describe the yellowing
of a leaf due to the destruction of chlorophyll or the
failure of chlorophyll to form. Why leaves lose or fail
to form chlorophyll can be attributed to many causes,
including poor drainage, damaged roots, compacted soil
and nutrient deficiencies, but it can also be a normal
occurrence in the life-cycle of a plant.**

Yellow leaves are often associated with overwatering, but as
you've come to learn through this book, it's not the volume of
water alone that causes a plant's roots to decay: how quickly
a plant is utilising water is dependent on how much light it is
receiving. An 'overwatered' plant is often one that's not being

Diagnose your plant

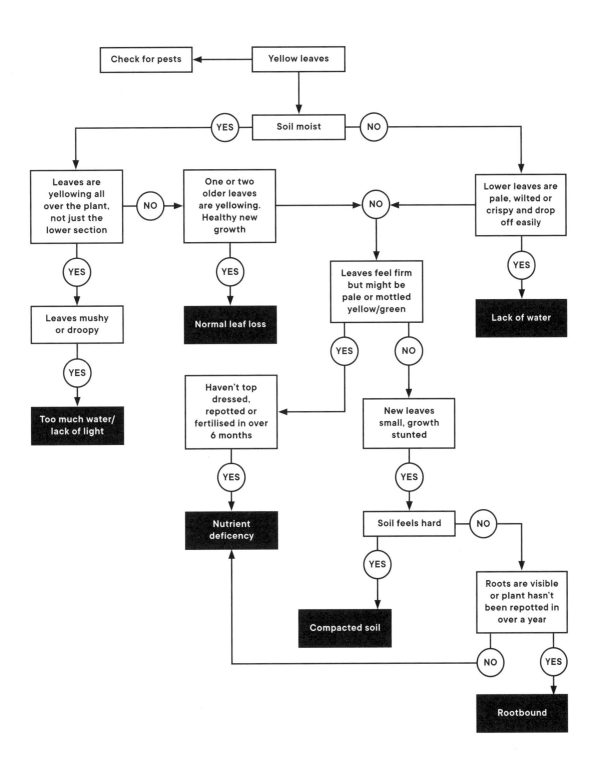

provided with enough light to be able to use the volume of water it's being given, and the result is that water remains in the soil for a prolonged period of time. Roots need oxygen to survive, which is why the soil should always be aerobic (full of air pockets), rather than anaerobic (void of oxygen because of too much water). The longer water remains in the soil, the longer the roots are starved of oxygen, and the greater the opportunity for bacteria to thrive and attack the roots.

Rescue suggestion
Check if there is water collecting in the decorative pot. If you have been watering without removing the plant from the decorative pot, water can collect at the bottom and lead to soggy soil. If there are only a handful of leaves that are yellowing, I suggest simply taking the inner pot out and moving it to a brighter position to allow the soil to completely dry. Place it in moderate to bright indirect light to kickstart the photosynthesis process, which will increase the uptake of moisture from the soil. Repotting is a stressful experience for an already unhappy plant, so it's best avoided if possible.

If the symptoms are severe, and more than a quarter of the leaves are yellow, remove the plant from its inner grow pot – this will give you an opportunity to confirm how much moisture is in the soil and also to check for rotten roots. Gently remove the soil so you are able to see the roots: they should be firm and a light cream or beige colour. If there is a distinctive damp smell and some of the roots are brown and mushy, they are rotting and not able to function properly. Hopefully not all will have rotted – check if there are any that look light in colour and still feel firm. If so, all is not lost.

— Using clean scissors, snip away any roots that have rotted, leaving only firm ones attached to the plant.
— Take the plant to the sink and rinse the remaining roots, you can also flush the roots with chamomile-infused water (see page 96). Leave to dry off.
— Depending on how much of the root ball has been lost you may choose to repot it in a smaller pot with fresh houseplant soil. If planting back in the original pot, make sure you thoroughly wash the pot before doing so.
— Do not water the plant straight after repotting as its roots need to recover.

— Your plant has been through a very stressful time and it needs to recover. Place it near a window that receives moderate to bright indirect light and be patient. Hold off on watering for at least a few days, then slowly begin to reintroduce water. Remember the root ball has been reduced in size, so the amount you water must also be reduced. Allow the soil to completely dry out before adding more water.
— The plant may look worse before it starts to look better – this is normal, try not to panic. What your plant wants more than anything right now is to be left alone. Recovery from severe root rot is not always possible. Only time will tell if it will make it.

Lack of water

Typically, lower leaves are affected first by lack of water. And plants suffering from a lack of water are more likely to develop yellow leaves in summer, rather than winter. As the light and temperature increase during spring and summer, plants become more active in their growth, which results in more water being used, reducing the risk of overwatering and increasing the risk of underwatering. This is a general observation, not a rule: yellow leaves can occur for either reason at any time of the year.

To check if the plant is yellowing due to lack of water, pick up the pot to feel if it is heavy or light. If the pot feels light, there probably isn't much moisture in the soil – to be sure, use your finger or a chopstick to check deep into the soil. Visual signs of very dry soil can be a gap between the soil and the pot edges, indicating the soil has contracted.

Rescue suggestion
— Take the plant in its inner grow pot to an empty sink with the plug in. Place the pot in the sink and turn on the tap – once the water reaches about halfway up the pot, turn off the tap and leave the plant to absorb the water for 10-15 minutes.
— Cut the yellow leaves off if you like, but it's not necessary.
— A plant that has not been able to access water has also not had access to the vital minerals and nutrients it needs, so next time you water, add some fertiliser (see 'nutrient deficiency' on the following page for more information on this).

Nutrient deficiency

If you have never (or rarely) added fertiliser to the soil, and you have also ruled out the possibilities of too much or too little water, as well as the plant being rootbound, it may be that your plant needs feeding. Leaves that are pale green-yellow or have yellow areas between the veins can be signs of deficiencies, and in some cases this can be combined with stunted growth.

Plants, like humans, can become deficient in vital minerals. Houseplant soil contains nutrients to supply the plant for around 3–6 months, but after this time you will need to add fertiliser during the plant's active growth period.

The three main elements required for growth are nitrogen, potassium and phosphorus, which are found in various ratios in most general plant fertilisers (see page 97).

Lack of nitrogen The plant can move nitrogen around, so if it has too little it will take it from the older leaves to supply it to the new growth. The result is that older leaves turn yellowish-green, with spindly stems and stunted new growth.

Lack of phosphorus You might notice stunted growth and older leaves turning darker green. A flowering plant may struggle to flower.

Lack of potassium The edges of older leaves can appear burnt because the plant's ability to regulate water is affected. Lower leaves typically turn yellow and growth is slow.

Rescue suggestion
The advice on when to feed your plant is usually, 'during the growing season in spring and summer', but if it's growing leaves in winter, it still needs fertiliser. However, if you are feeding it outside of the traditional growing period, I suggest diluting it to half the strength. If you are using grow lights, you must also feed your plant as it is always in active growth. If you don't want to add fertiliser you can top dress the soil.

Rootbound

A rootbound or pot-bound plant is likely to be suffering from a lack of water and vital nutrients, so the signs will be similar to those of a plant starved of these vital elements. Pale or yellow leaves can occur in both young and old leaves, and the lower leaves may appear brown or wilted, which is consistent with the signs of a thirsty plant. Growth may also be stunted. See page 93 for signs that your plant needs to be potted on.

Rescue suggestion
Check the plant roots by taking it out of the inner grow pot: if they are circling around the bottom of the pot, it needs to be potted on into a larger pot (see page 94).

Compacted soil

Soil becomes compacted when the roots are constantly absorbing moisture. Compacted soil inhibits the movement of water, oxygen and nutrients, which makes it difficult for the roots to function efficiently, resulting in yellow leaves and stunted growth.

It's very important to regularly check the soil for signs of compaction and address the issue before it has a detrimental effect on the plant. It may not be possible to easily push your finger or a chopstick into compacted soil, which points to the conclusion that the plant's roots haven't been able to access enough water. You may dismiss the idea that your plant is suffering from a lack of water if you've been watering regularly, but if the soil is compacted then that water may not have been reaching all the roots. Signs of compacted soil also include very dry soil and a gap between the soil and the pot.

Rescue suggestion
A plant that has been in the same soil for a year or more that has become compacted is probably best removed and repotted in fresh potting mix. If you would rather not repot it, aerate the soil and then top dress it. Aeration can be achieved with a pencil, chopstick or anything that you can push into the soil to create narrow holes. Making channels allows oxygen and water to flow more freely. After aerating, add some fresh potting mix on top and then water thoroughly. It's good practice to aerate every time you water a plant.

Normal leaf loss

It's important to remember that some symptoms that look alarming are just part of the normal life-cycle of a plant. A plant discarding one or two older leaves is normal. But if this is happening frequently, or the younger leaves are affected, then it's likely a problem. (See Leaf Drop on page 199.)

Pest damage

See page 216.

Wilting

A lack of water and too much water can, confusingly, both cause a plant to look wilted. This is why taking time to investigate further is essential.

When we see a wilted plant, our immediate assumption is that it must be thirsty, and in a way we're right – but not necessarily because we've underwatered it. A plant can be thirsty even if it's drowning in water. If the roots have rotted, they are unable to supply the plant with water, so it wilts. It's the water pressure within the cells of the plant that helps them stand upright. When the cells aren't provided with water, they shrink, and this causes the plant to wilt.

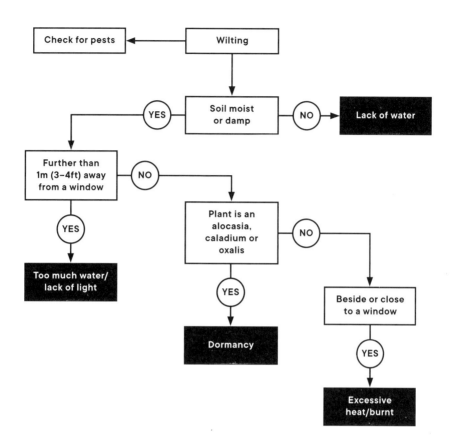

**Too much water/
lack of light**

How quickly a plant is utilising water is dependent on how much light it is receiving and the health of its roots. A lack of oxygen in the soil combined with an overgrowth of bacteria (caused by water remaining in the soil for a prolonged period) causes the roots to decay and eventually die. The plant may continue to survive even though a proportion of the roots have started to rot, but it won't look healthy. The supply of water to the plant reduces with every root that dies.

Rescue suggestion
If the entire plant has wilted, the root system is severely and possibly terminally damaged. The only way to check how badly affected the roots are is to remove the plant from the inner grow pot and inspect them. They should be firm and a light cream or beige colour; if some of them are brown and mushy, they have rotted and need to be cut away. If all the

roots feel mushy and are black-brown, then I'm afraid I must refer you to the section 'when it's time to say goodbye' on page 168.

If some of the roots are firm and lighter in colour there is hope that the plant may live, but it's a 50/50 chance. You must perform the potentially life-saving rescue suggestion outlined in Yellow Leaves under 'too much water/lack of light' (see page 170).

Lack of water

During a drought plants go into crisis mode and begin shutting down to conserve what little water is left. Stomata are closed to keep moisture from escaping, but this also means CO_2 can't be absorbed, which is essential for photosynthesis. The plant stops making food, while the lack of water causes the cells to deflate, which results in a wilted appearance. Depending on the type of plant and how long it has been without access to water, recovery may or may not be possible. There is only one way to find out...

Rescue suggestion

Well, this is an obvious one – water it. Take the plant in its grow pot to the sink (if you are able to) and pour water slowly into the soil. If it is rolling off the soil and over the pot's rim (rather than sinking in), use a pencil or chopstick to drive holes into the soil to help the water reach the roots. Keep pouring in water until the soil is saturated. You can also sit the pot in a shallow tub of water so the moisture can be absorbed from the bottom. Leave the plant in the water for 20–30 minutes, then set it aside to drain before returning it to the decorative pot. Cut off any brown crispy leaves and wait for signs of recovery.

If your plant looks very badly wilted (i.e. it has a brown stem and all the leaves are brown), you might want to do an experiment to see if it's dead or can be saved.

— If the stem is brown, use your fingernail to scrape it: the hope is that you see some green underneath. Stems should be pliable and firm, not brittle and brown like a stick.
— Take the plant out of the grow pot: the roots, like the stem, should be firm and pliable rather than brittle. If the roots are brittle this is not a good sign.

If the stem and all the leaves are brown, but the roots are still firm and pliable, it's possible to try to save the plant.

— The aim is to remove any part of the plant that is dead. Cut the stem back, feeling as you go. Sometimes the stem may feel more pliable the nearer to the roots you get. You may end up cutting most of the stem, but try to leave at least 5–7.5cm (2–3in) above the roots or a node.
— Pot the plant in fresh free-draining houseplant soil.
— Water generously, until the soil is completely saturated. Put the plant somewhere bright, but not in direct sunlight or anywhere excessively warm.
— Keep checking the soil, adding water only when it is approaching dry.
— If there is no new growth in 8–10 weeks, you can assume the plant is completely dead
— If there is new growth, throw a welcome party and invite everyone you know around to admire the new bit of stem.

Excessive heat/burnt

Broadly speaking, plants with dark green leaves are more able to absorb light and therefore better able to adapt to shade and low light. Placing a tropical plant with dark green leaves beside a very bright, south-facing window in summer is likely to end badly, particularly if the leaves are thin and easily damaged. A tropical plant placed next to a window with direct sunlight in summer will feel like it is participating in a marathon through Death Valley without suncream. As much as I bang on about giving your plants light, excessive light (directly hitting the leaves) can be extremely damaging to many of the most common indoor plants, resulting in wilted or burnt leaves.

Most plants (apart from the woody ones) are able to stand because of water pressure and they are constantly regulating the loss of water by opening and closing their stomata; the more light (and heat) the plant receives, the faster the rate of photosynthesis and transpiration (water release) through the stomata. If the amount of water lost is more than the plant can keep up with by absorbing it through its roots, the plant will lose pressure and wilt.

Sunlight can also burn the leaves, damaging the chlorophyll and resulting in bleached areas which can be white, yellow or brown.

Rescue suggestion

Check the soil for moisture. If the soil is moist, it could be that the plant was simply unable to keep up with the amount of water it was losing versus how much the roots were able to absorb. Move the plant at least 60–90cm (2–3ft) back from the window and let it recover. Burnt areas will not repair themselves, but you can leave them or cut off the leaf.

If the soil is dry, the plant needs urgent hydration. Follow the rescue suggestion for a 'lack of water' on page 173. Find a new position for the plant that receives less intense light.

Dormancy

For plants living outdoors, dormancy can be part of a seasonal life-cycle. For plants living indoors, dormancy isn't always an obvious event: some plants will simply show slow growth or stop putting on new growth, while others might show more visible signs. If a caladium, oxalis or alocasia is losing most of its leaves without producing more, it's likely moving into dormancy. Members of the *Calathea* genus, such as the popular prayer plant, may also go fully dormant. If all the leaves become brown and crispy, but the roots are healthy, don't throw it away, it might just need to rest before regrowing.

Dormancy can be brought on by a drop in temperature, lack of water or poor light levels. If the plant is still producing new leaves while shedding lower leaves, don't worry, this is a normal part of its life-cycle.

Rescue suggestion

To establish whether your plant is unwell or becoming dormant, gently remove it from the grow pot and look at its roots: healthy roots should look light cream or beige and feel firm, rotting roots will be mushy, and dead roots will be brown, crispy and brittle.

If the roots are healthy but the leaves are drooping, you have two choices: give the plant more light and see if it perks up (remember more light will mean the plant will use more water); or alternatively, allow the plant to go dormant naturally. To do the latter, reduce watering (by at least 50%) and allow it to lose its leaves and then follow one of the two options on the following page. If the roots are rotten but the tubers are still firm, all is not lost. You can store the tubers and try growing the plant again in spring following one of these two options.

Option 1 Leave the tubers in the pot. Stop watering the plant and place the pot somewhere cool and in low light. Leave it there over autumn and winter. Bring the pot out in spring, or earlier if you see new growth, and put it in a warm bright place and resume watering. Only water the plant a little and allow the soil to dry out before watering again.

Option 2 Remove the tubers from the pot and store them over winter. This is a good option if the roots have rotted. There is a small risk that the tubers will shrivel up during storage and may not grow again, but with any luck they will be fine.
— Remove the plant from the pot and remove all the soil until you can see the tubers.
— Cut back the leaves and the roots and set the tubers aside to dry out for a week.
— Brush all the dry soil off the tubers and place them in a cardboard box filled with shredded paper. Leave the box somewhere cool over winter.
— Spring is the best time to wake up the tubers (caladiums need the temperature to be at least 20°C before they will sprout).
— Fill a pot with a free-draining potting mix and moisten it using a spray bottle. Place the tubers in the soil (caladium tubers have a smooth bottom and bumpy top, but don't worry if you put them in upside down they will still grow).
— Cover them with around 4cm (1.5in) of soil and lightly mist the soil to moisten. Put the pot somewhere warm and bright. Spritz the soil occasionally to keep it lightly moistened, but not damp or wet.
— Placing a cloche or clear plastic bag over the pot can help to create a greenhouse effect and raise the humidity, but take it off once every 3–4 days to allow fresh air to circulate. Remove when you see growth.
— When you start to see growth, which can take 1–2 months, add a small amount of general fertiliser to the water once every few weeks.

Pest damage   See page 216.

Leaning

A plant that is leaning may be doing so because it is top heavy and unable to support itself. If this is the case, add a stake to support it in a more upright position. Leaning is also a plant's natural response to light that is coming from one side, rather than from above. Alternatively, the roots may be rotting.

Phototropism

Plants have responses to various stimuli such as water, light, gravity and touch, which are referred to as 'tropisms'. A plant's response to light is called phototropism and can be negative (growing away from light) or positive (growing towards light). Roots grow away from light and the stem grows towards it.

Auxins are plant hormones that are predominantly

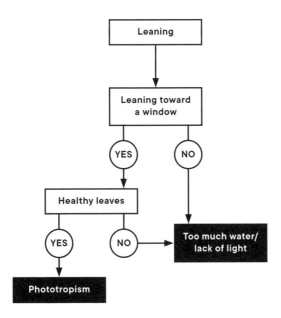

made in the tips of growing stems and roots. When the photoreceptors in plant cells detect light, auxins in the stem are sent in the direction of that light. When light comes from above, auxins are spread equally at the tip and down both sides of the stem, but when the light comes from the side, auxins cause the cells on the shaded side to elongate and to point the plant in the direction of the light. Your plant isn't technically bending towards the light, the stem is growing unequally because the light is hitting it less on one side than the other. In simple terms, if your plant is leaning, it's responding to the light in an unbalanced way.

Rescue suggestion

Ideally you want the plant to be growing straight upwards, so in order to counteract the lean, turn the pot the opposite way, so that it is pointing away from the light – in a few days the plant will begin to lean towards the direction of the light and in doing so, will slowly straighten up. To avoid the same thing happening again, turn the pot regularly, about once a week. Leaning can be caused by a lack of light, so experiment with moving the plant closer to a window. Alternatively, consider placing it under a grow light so it grows straight upwards towards the light above.

**Too much water/
lack of light**

Although not an obvious symptom, leaning can be caused by root rot, which is brought about by too much water and a lack of light. Rotting roots, rather than plump and firm roots, become mushy and are no longer able to support the plant, which potentially results in the plant collapsing.

Rescue suggestion

If you suspect you may have been adding too much water, remove the plant from its grow pot and inspect the roots. If the soil is soggy and the roots look brown and mushy, follow the rescue suggestion outlined in Yellow Leaves under 'too much water/lack of light' (see page 170).

Stretching/Elongating

Spindly, leggy, pale, weak stems (often with small leaves that are far apart) or long, puny, thin growth on cacti are indicators of what's known as 'etiolation'. Etiolation occurs when a plant isn't receiving enough light and is 'reaching' for light. It is a common problem seen in succulents, cacti and vining plants, particularly when there are seasonal changes in light levels.

In nature a plant will receive signals from a seasonal drop in light, temperature and water to become dormant. Indoors, a houseplant continues to receive warmth and water, but experiences lower light levels, so it is effectively stretching to find light in an attempt to continue growing.

Some plants, particularly succulents, often grow leggy as they mature. Mature succulents that are leggy, but are otherwise vibrant with plump, regular leaves, are nothing to worry about and can look characterful. But if you want your succulents to keep their compact shape, place them in a bright position. If you have run out of space near the brightest window, consider getting a grow light as this opens up more opportunities for plants to live all around the house, not just beside the windows.

Rescue suggestion

The simple solution to etiolation is to give the plant more light, but this is like closing the door after the horse has bolted – a stretched plant won't revert to normal just by giving it more light. Instead, you can opt to cut the plant back and place it in a position with more light.

If you choose to chop an etoilated succulent:
— Use a clean pair of small sharp scissors or a knife.
— Cut the etiolated stem off (new pups will hopefully emerge).
— If you choose, you can propagate the piece you cut off (see page 233).

If you choose to chop an etiolated foliage plant:
— Cut the stem where it has become bare and the leaves are smaller than the rest of the plant.
— If you choose, you can propagate the piece you cut off (see page 230).

Brown Leaves

Plants grow new leaves and shed older ones as part of their natural life-cycle – it's a way of conserving energy and is nothing to worry about. If you see a few of the older leaves occasionally shrivelling up, but new growth is healthy with no other signs of browning or yellowing, you can probably relax.

As with yellow leaves (see page 170), if there's a problem at play, it's most likely caused by an issue with watering, but brown leaves can also indicate a variety of other problems.

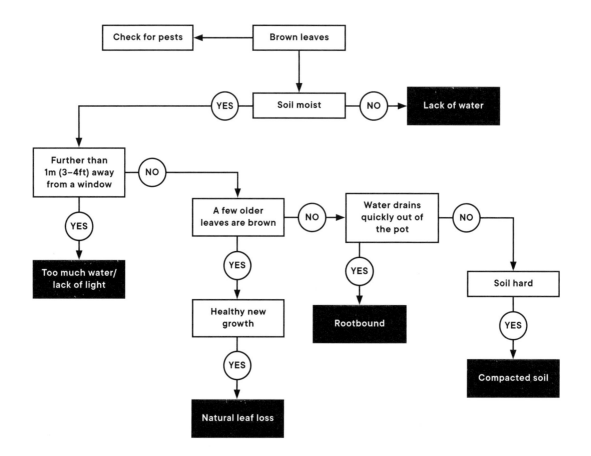

Lack of water

Brown leaves can be the result of the soil being too dry. They can also indicate that a plant's roots are unable to keep up with the amount of water being lost through the leaves (transpiration). Increased light and warmer temperatures in the summer can speed up the process of transpiration, so soil dries out faster than in cooler months. Lack of water will often cause leaves to curl and then become crinkly and fall off.

Rescue suggestion

If only a few leaves have turned brown, take the plant to the sink and give the soil a thorough soak. After fully saturating the soil, move the plant to a position that allows it to access bright indirect light. Cut off the brown leaves. Don't be tempted to keep adding water every day in a bid to revive it; let it use up the water in the soil before adding more.

If more than half of the leaves have turned brown see the rescue suggestion outlined in Wilting under 'lack of water' (see page 178).

Too much water/ lack of light

Leaves that turn crispy and brown may point to damage caused to the roots by excessive watering and a lack of light. The symptoms of rotting roots can be exactly the same as the symptoms of lack of water, as damaged roots cannot supply the plant with the water it needs to function.

Rescue suggestion
Follow the rescue suggestion outlined in Yellow Leaves under 'too much water/lack of light' (see page 170).

Rootbound

A rootbound plant has outgrown its pot, filling all the available space with roots. Signs that a plant needs a bigger pot are numerous: water that drains quickly out of the pot (indicative of there not being much soil); roots growing out of the bottom of the drainage holes; and yellow or brown leaves, usually on the lower portion of the plant.

Rescue suggestion
See page 174 for further symptoms of a rootbound plant and advice on how to remedy the problem.

Compacted soil

Hard, compacted soil can inhibit the roots' ability to access water – if the soil particles are compacted, water can't properly penetrate the soil, which may result in some leaves wilting and turning brown.

Rescue suggestion
Follow the rescue suggestions outlined in Yellow Leaves under 'compacted soil' (see page 175).

Pest damage

See page 216.

Brown or Black Leaf Margins/Tips

Areas where living cells and tissue have degenerated and turned brown or black are referred to as 'necrosis'. These areas of the plant have died and can't be revived. Necrosis weakens the plant, making it more susceptible to pests and disease. Once the tips of a leaf have turned brown they won't turn green again. If it bothers you, you can trim the brown bits off, but try to follow the shape of the leaf to give a more natural look. I would recommend leaving them.

Lack of water

The tips of the leaf are a plant's extremities, much like our fingertips and toes. When a plant is stressed by a lack of water, the leaf tips, being the last to receive it, are the first

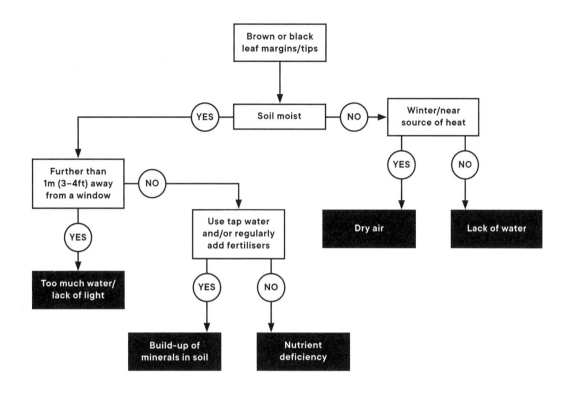

casualty. Brown tips can be an early warning that there is an issue with watering. It only takes one period of drought to cause damage to the leaf tips; if the dry spell continues, the damage can spread.

Rescue suggestion
Look for reasons the plant may be suffering from lack of water:
— Have you forgotten to water it? When was the last time you checked the soil for moisture?
— Is the soil compacted? See 'compacted soil' under Yellow Leaves on page 175.
— Is the plant rootbound? See 'rootbound' under Yellow Leaves on page 174.
— Is the potting mix suitable for the particular plant? It could be too free-draining, meaning the water is not being retained. See Houseplant Soil on page 80 for ideas on how to increase water retention.

Too much water/ lack of light

Plants show stress by changes in their appearance. The most common cause of stress is an issue with watering – either too little or too much in relation to the amount of light the plant is receiving. While yellow/brown leaves can be a major cry for help, brown tips can be an early warning sign that something isn't working as it should – it could be a lack of water in the soil or it could be roots that aren't functioning due to root rot.

Rescue suggestion

Check the soil to establish how moist it is. Then consider the position of your plant and whether it is receiving enough light. Experiment with moving it to a brighter position so it's better able to utilise the water it's receiving. If you choose to leave it in low light, you must reduce the amount of water you are giving the plant.

Check the roots, they should be light cream or beige in colour and feel firm. If any are mushy and brown, follow the rescue suggestion outlined in Yellow Leaves under 'too much water/lack of light' (see page 170).

Build-up of minerals in the soil

Adding fertiliser and tap water to soil can over time lead to a build-up of minerals that may become toxic to the plant. Among the chemicals found in tap water are fluoride and chlorine; at low levels these aren't toxic, and in fact chlorine is a micronutrient, but a build-up in the soil can cause salinity stress resulting in brown leaf tips. An excessive accumulation of fluoride is commonly reported to affect dracaenas, calatheas and the spider plant. Carnivorous plants are highly sensitive to tap water and it can cause them to die – never use tap water for these plants.

Roots absorb water and minerals from the soil, which are transported upwards and around the plant. The leaf tip is the last to receive this supply, and if the concentration of minerals is high, the build-up of salts can cause the tips to burn. Excessive minerals in the soil can also cause roots to shrivel, making them more susceptible to disease and inhibiting their ability to absorb water. If too much fertiliser is the cause of brown tips, you may see the marginal browning separated from the rest of the leaf by a slender yellow hue.

If you don't like the look of the brown tips, you can trim them off, but try to follow the shape of the leaf to give a more natural look.

Rescue suggestions

If you've been adding fertiliser or tap water to your plant over a long period of time, you may notice a crust has formed on the surface of the soil. If this is the case, remove the top few centimetres of soil and discard. Then flush the soil with the purest water you have access to (rainwater, or water from an aquarium, air-conditioning unit or dehumidifier). Pour in more water than you normally would when watering, as the aim is to flush out the excess minerals. Let the water totally drain away before top dressing with fresh potting mix and placing the plant in moderate to bright light.

Commercial fertiliser is highly concentrated, so be extremely careful when diluting it. To reduce the risk of burning your plants' roots, fertilise when the soil is moist and dilute the fertiliser with double the recommended amount of water, which makes it half the recommended strength. For more, see Plant Food on page 97.

Some people choose to let tap water sit in a watering can overnight before using it to water their plants. While the chlorine within the water will dissipate somewhat, chloramine (a group of chemical compounds that contain chlorine and ammonia) won't dissipate, so actually leaving water to sit doesn't make it any more pure. Using tap water is generally fine, as long as you flush the soil (as outlined above) with a purer water every once in a while.

Nutrient deficiency

If the area of the leaf was yellow before turning brown/black, this could be a symptom of a mineral/nutrient deficiency caused by a lack of potassium, calcium, chlorine or sodium.

Rescue suggestion

Look for reasons the plant may be suffering from a deficiency:
— Has the plant been in the same soil for more than a year without receiving any fertiliser? If so, it's likely to be lacking in vital nutrients.
— Is the plant rootbound? See page 93.
— Has the soil degraded or become compacted? Aerate the soil by using a chopstick to create channels, then saturate the plant with water and leave for a few days before adding fertiliser. Alternatively, consider repotting if the soil looks old and spent.

Dry air/lack of humidity

Dry warm air (effectively a lack of humidity) is often assumed to be the cause of brown leaf margins. Tropical plants are native to environments with high humidity levels, but they can adapt fairly quickly to the humidity levels in our homes. Calatheas are particularly prone to suffering from brown margins on the leaves, but this isn't usually down to lack of humidity alone, other factors (including those mentioned on the previous pages) are likely to be contributing to the problem. In winter, central heating causes the air to become drier than it is in the spring and summer. When the air is dry and warm (as opposed to humid and warm), transpiration of water from the leaf is more rapid. Slowing the rate of transpiration by increasing the humidity surrounding the plant could be an option.

Rescue suggestion
In winter, move plants away from sources of heat such as radiators and open fires. If you have underfloor heating, raise them up off the floor on a stand. If you want to experiment with increasing the humidity, use a humidifier (see page 74). If the plant is reasonably small, you could try covering it with a cloche or adding it to a terrarium.

Curling Leaves

A plant is constantly working to regulate the amount of water needed for survival. Like human sweat glands, the stomata are responsible for releasing excess moisture through transpiration, which helps to cool the plant. Stomata need to be open to allow CO_2 absorption, but if they need to limit moisture loss, they can close. There is another trick the plant can perform to reduce loss of water, which is curling its leaves inwards. Stomata are mostly found on the undersides of leaves, so by rolling inwards the plant can hold on to moisture by creating a humid mini-microclimate inside the curled-up leaf. This can often be seen when prayer plants are thirsty or suffering from a lack of humidity. Plants may also curl their leaves if they are receiving too much light, as this allows them to reduce the surface area exposed to light.

Rescue suggestion

Curling leaves are most commonly a sign that the plant needs water. Fully saturate the soil with water and allow it to flow out of the drainage holes. Monitor how quickly moisture disappears from the soil after watering. It could be the plant is using it more quickly than you thought, particularly if the intensity of light is very bright. Since transpiration increases in dry air, ensure the plant isn't sitting near a source of heat, such as a radiator. Look for reasons the plant may be suffering from lack of water:

— Is the soil suitable for the particular plant? It could be too free-draining, meaning the water is not being retained. See Houseplant Soil on page 80 for ideas on how to increase water retention.

— Is the soil compacted? See 'compacted soil' under Yellow Leaves on page 175.

— Is the plant rootbound? See 'rootbound' under Yellow Leaves on page 174.

Brown Circular Spots

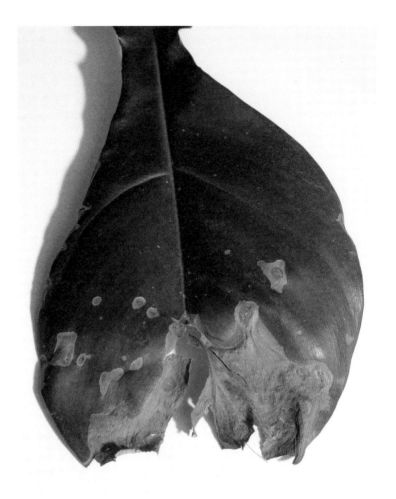

Bacterial and fungal spores love a moist environment.
Giving your plant water when it's not receiving enough
light allows moisture to remain in the potting mix and
creates an inviting environment for bacteria to grow.
You don't want a plant sitting in moist soil in low light as
this will quickly become a bacteria hotel; the idea isn't
to treat the bacteria well, it's to treat the plant well. Make
it harder for bacteria to grow by sticking with the rules of
LAW (see page 72) and you will reduce the risk of bacterial
and fungal infections.

Fungal infection	Clues that the plant has a fungal infection include brown spots with a yellow outline (though be aware, it could still be fungal without the yellow outline), and brown spots that look papery and thin. These spots can grow together and cause large areas of the leaf to turn brown. Leaf spots can occur when fungal spores find a warm, humid area to grow. Spots can occur on any leaf including new growth and may spread to other parts of the plant.

Rescue suggestions
— Leaves infected with fungal spots should be cut off to minimise the spread of the infection. If plants are grouped closely together, move them apart to increase air flow and to minimise the risk of others in your collection becoming infected.
— Take care not to get the foliage wet when watering. Keep the soil free from fallen leaves where bacteria can grow.
— If you are misting a plant to clean it, use a cloth to wipe away the excess moisture. I don't suggest misting calatheas, as these plants are particularly prone to fungal leaf spot. Don't mist any plants that have hairy leaves, such as begonias, which are prone to powdery mildew.
— Treat the plant with an organic fungicidal spray.
— If it is in low light, move it to a brighter position so the water in the soil can be used up at a faster rate, or alternatively water it less. Since excessive moisture in the soil is the cause of an overgrowth of bacteria, it's worth checking the roots of the plant to see if they have signs of root rot, and then follow the rescue suggestion outlined in Yellow Leaves under 'too much water/lack of light' (see page 170).

Pest damage	See page 216.

Leaf Drop

Leaf loss is a normal part of the life-cycle of a plant. It's unsustainable for a plant to keep all its leaves for its entire life, so they are discarded when they are no longer needed and new ones form.

There are occasions when a plant will drop leaves because something has gone wrong with its care. This can be a gradual loss, brought about by something as simple as a lack of light, or a sudden loss.

When plants go into shock, they are basically in panic mode. Something about their environment has suddenly changed and it can cause an extreme reaction. Discarding leaves is a simple, quick and effective way for the plant to

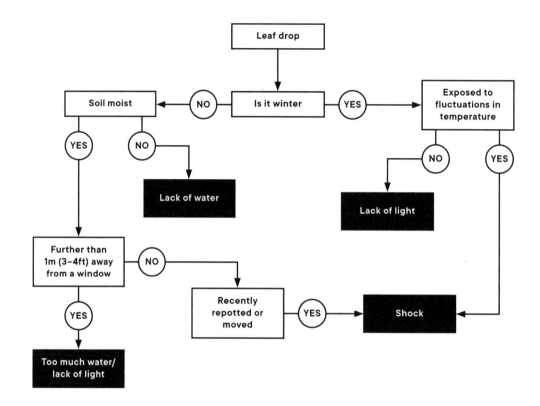

conserve resources and you'll likely see sudden leaf loss. The shock can be caused by a change in light, temperature or water supply. Identifying which of these environmental conditions have been changed should be easy, but only you will know how, when and why this happened.

Lack of light

Gradual leaf loss can happen during winter, most likely brought on by a lack of light.

Rescue suggestion

Move the plant to a brighter position, close to a window, but make sure it is not beside a radiator. Alternatively, buy a grow light. I have lots of grow lights on through the winter months to keep my plants healthy. Remember, when light intensity is increased, water should be too.

Change in temperature or environment

Tropical plants have a limited ability to adapt to temperature extremes, which makes them vulnerable to a sudden drop in temperature. A sudden change in temperature can affect plant metabolism: cold can inhibit photosynthesis and decrease water uptake, which can cause cells to shrink and collapse, resulting in leaf loss.

A change in environment (such as moving house) can result in a sudden drop in temperature, it could also mean the plant is newly in a position with more or less light. Some plants, such as the weeping fig and fiddle leaf fig, are more sensitive to changes in their environment than others.

Rescue suggestion

The recovery of a plant that has dropped all or most of its leaves due to shock is 50/50. There isn't much you can do other than wait to see if it recovers. Make sure it's in a position that isn't draughty or near a radiator, and that has moderate to bright indirect light. Only water the plant when the soil is approaching dry. Don't fuss over it. Leaving it alone to recover is the best option. If no signs of recovery are visible in 6–8 weeks, it might be time to say goodbye (see page 168).

Inconsistent watering

Plants rely on water to remain turgid. If the plant doesn't receive enough water, the cells within the plant shrink and the plant wilts, and leaves will die and drop off. This can happen because the roots are damaged by too much water (and not enough light), or because the soil is dry. You may also notice brown patches on the leaves. Inconsistent watering or a sudden change in the amount of water the plant is receiving can result in shock.

Rescue suggestion

Follow the rescue suggestion in Yellow Leaves under either 'too much water/lack of light' or 'lack of water' (see page 170).

Repotting

Some plants can suffer shock after being repotted. This can be because the flow of water was temporarily cut off (while the roots were out of soil), or the tiny root hairs were damaged while the plant was being removed from the soil.

Rescue suggestion

Always remove a plant from its pot carefully to minimise root disturbance or damage. You don't need to remove all the soil from the roots when repotting, unless you are treating root rot or pests. The less you poke around the roots the better.

If after repotting the plant is losing leaves, try not to panic. Doing anything to the plant while it's in a state of shock rarely ends well. Don't be tempted to repot again, move it to a new location or keep pouring in more water. You have to leave it alone to adjust. Fussing will only result in more stress and more leaf loss. Within a week or two, the plant should have adapted to the change and show signs of stabilisation.

If you are left with only a few leaves, for example on a fiddle leaf fig, you may consider notching the stem. Notching or nicking a woody stem can encourage new leaves to grow and potentially even some branching. Do this in spring when the plant is likely to be in its growing period.

— Locate an area of stem that is between two nodes.
— Using a clean knife, score a cut with a downward angle into the stem. Make it 2–5mm deep and ensure the cut covers about one third of the circumference of the stem. The white sticky sap is normal and you can wipe it off.
— Make another cut with an upward angle directly underneath the first one. Make it about 1–2mm deep. The idea is to join the two cuts together to make the shape of a mouth on the stem. Then peel back the woody top layer to expose the creamy-white tissue.
— Leave it and see if a leaf bud forms – it could take 1–3 months. If it doesn't, try again in another area on the stem; there is a 50% success rate.

You could take drastic action by chopping the stem back, which can promote new leaf growth further down the stem. This is best done in spring. You can also propagate the top part of the plant.

— Decide where to cut the stem; I would suggest no further than halfway down.
— If your plant has sap that is a potential irritant (such as a ficus) wear gloves. Make a cut using clean secateurs (the cut may ooze white sap); keep children and pets away.
— Place the remaining plant in bright indirect light (light is absolutely key for leaves to regrow).
— Water when the soil is dry. Bear in mind that the plant has no (or few) leaves so it's not going to be using up the water quickly. Always check the soil before watering.
— When leaves appear, water with a tiny amount of very diluted fertiliser.

Stunted Growth/Small or Deformed Leaves

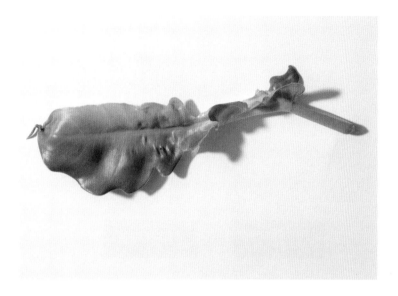

A plant lacking in energy will not grow properly. Low energy can result in weak, spindly, elongated stems, small leaves or no growth at all. Plants growing in poor environmental conditions (such as low light or poor soil) can also experience stunted growth. Stunted growth often shows up with other symptoms, most commonly yellow leaves (see page 170).

Lack of light

A common reason for a plant producing small leaves is a lack of light. Energy, in the form of sunlight, is one of the driving forces in photosynthesis. A plant producing small leaves doesn't have the energy to produce full-size leaves. This characteristic can be combined with an elongating stem and larger spaces between leaf nodes. During winter, plants may often produce small leaves due to a drop in the amount of light available.

Rescue suggestion

Just because a room looks bright does not mean your plant is receiving bright light. Move the plant closer to a window and you should see new growth with the leaf size returning to normal. Remember, the more light the plant receives, the more water it will use.

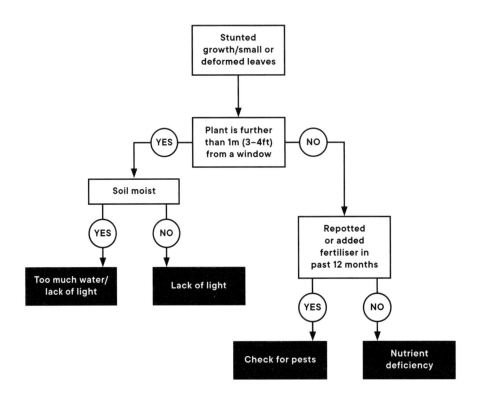

**Too much water/
lack of light**

An interruption in the supply of water and nutrients through the roots can affect the plant's ability to photosynthesise efficiently, and the deficiency becomes apparent in the condition of the foliage. Too much water in the soil can lead to a lack of oxygen and build-up of bacteria, which then results in root rot; the plant is left struggling, unable to grow properly.

Rescue suggestion
If you suspect the soil has become waterlogged, follow the rescue suggestion in Yellow Leaves under 'too much water/ lack of light' (see page 170).

Nutrient deficiency

Small, pale or yellowing leaves can be a symptom that the plant is lacking in nutrients.

Rescue suggestion
Over time, soil is depleted of nutrients. You may decide to refresh the soil by either repotting the plant (see page 94) or aerating the soil then top dressing it with fresh soil. If you don't want to repot the plant, feed it with fertiliser,

taking care to follow the dilution recommendations. For more, see 'nutrient deficiency' under Yellow Leaves (see page 174).

Pests

In my experience, most leaf deformities (and occasionally stunted growth) are caused by pests.

Rescue suggestion
See page 216 to help you identify and deal with pests.

White Powder on Leaves

Powdery mildew is a fungal disease that looks like a dusting of powder on infected leaves. Begonias are particularly susceptible, as are African violets. Powdery mildew inhibits the plant's ability to photosynthesise and can lead to an overall decline in health.

Rescue suggestion
If you spot powdery mildew:
—   Remove the infected leaves immediately.
—   Make a 50/50 solution of water and surgical spirit (rubbing alcohol).
—   Gently wipe or spray the remaining leaves with the solution.

Other suggestions include making a solution comprising bicarbonate of soda (1 tsp), castile soap (½ tsp) and water (500ml). Wipe or spray the leaves with the solution. After treating the plant, increase the air flow by moving it away from other plants. Repeat the treatment if you see signs of spores.

Loss of Variegation

Variegated plants have become a bit of an obsession amongst the houseplant community, with some species commanding extortionate prices. There are different types of variegation and one of the most unpredictable is chimeric variegation, which refers to a plant that has two genetically different types of cells. Popular mutations can be white, pink, orange or red, but they are random and unstable, and there are no guarantees that the plant will continue to produce variegated leaves. Be warned variegation lovers: if you don't provide the correct environment for these plants, they can revert to one colour, which can be a plant survival technique. Variegated areas of the leaf may also suffer from premature browning.

Lack of light

The leaves of some variegated plants, such as the popular *Monstera deliciosa* 'Albo-Variegata', have less surface area to capture light due to lower chlorophyll production in the variegated areas. Plants such as these need a brighter intensity of light than their green counterparts in order to compensate for this, and they will also grow more slowly as a result.

For a plant in low light, growing new leaves that aren't variegated is a way of indicating that the situation is unsustainable. The plant relies on the green areas of its leaves to capture the light for photosynthesis; chloroplasts are where photosynthesis takes place, and in low light, plants need to produce more chlorophyll in order to survive, which means more green and less variegation.

It's worth noting that naturally (genetically) variegated plants, such as the croton (*Codiaeum variegatum*), may also lose their variegation due to lack of light.

Rescue suggestion

If your plant is losing variegation, you need to move it to a brighter spot, closer to a window that receives bright light. If your home is lacking in good natural light, especially in winter, you might want to consider buying a grow light for your variegated plant. If you are unhappy with the loss of variegation, you can cut the plant back to the point where there is good variegation in the stem (this doesn't apply to naturally variegated plants such as the croton). Make the cut just above a node. Don't throw away the piece you cut off, propagate it instead (see page 230).

Too much water/ lack of light

A variegated plant can revert to green due to root rot. If the roots are damaged the plant will be stressed and may not produce further variegated leaves. As with all plants, getting the balance of light and water right is essential for maintaining healthy growth. A variegated plant has the same watering needs as a green plant.

Rescue suggestion

If you suspect root rot, follow the rescue suggestion in Yellow Leaves under 'too much water/lack of light' (see page 170). It's worth checking whether the soil is right for this type of plant – it shouldn't be overly dense. A medium that improves air flow while also retaining moisture is essential (see page 80).

White Mould on Soil

Pathogens, bacteria and fungal spores are present in all soil, but an overgrowth can occur if the environment is made too appealing for them. Saprophytic fungal spores can develop on the surface of the soil, and although it's harmless, it can be a sign of a problem with moisture remaining in the soil for a prolonged period of time due to lack of light and/or cold temperatures.

Rescue suggestion
First deal with the mould:
— Scoop out the top few centimetres of soil.
— Top up the soil level with fresh potting mix.
— If the mould returns, remove all of the old soil and repot the plant into fresh soil.

The mould is likely to be due to the potting mix remaining moist for long enough to encourage its growth. If the plant is in low light, reduce watering, but preferably move the plant to a brighter position so the water uptake is increased. Low light and lower temperatures in winter can cause moisture to remain in the soil for longer, so reduce watering in winter.

Flowerless Moth Orchid

Moth orchids (see page 134) are a victim of their own beauty: they are bought by retailers and customers when they are in bloom and discarded when they finish flowering. I urge you all to buy the ones with the wilting flowers before they are thrown away. Not only are they usually discounted, allowing you to buy three or four for the price of one, but if you give them just a small amount of care and attention, they will reward you with blooms for years to come.

Here's what to do when the flowers wilt and turn brown:
— If the flower spike hasn't turned brown and brittle, run your fingers down from the lowest flower until you locate a node (where growth emerges from the stem – it feels like a bump). Cut just above the node. Sometimes this encourages the plant to grow another flower spike from this point.
— If the flower spike is dead (i.e. it is brown and withered), cut it off at its base.
— Check to see if the plant needs repotting. If it's tightly rootbound, repot it into a larger pot using orchid bark – never use ordinary houseplant soil, as orchids are epiphytes and use their roots to absorb moisture from the bark of trees, rather than soil.
— Give all the leaves a wipe with a damp cloth to ensure they are free from dust.
— In summer, make sure it receives bright indirect light. In winter, a south-facing window is a good spot for it. An orchid can flower at almost any time of the year and light is key to this happening.
— Keep the roots hydrated by soaking the pot in water (see page 65). Allow the bark to completely dry out before watering again.
— During spring and summer, add orchid feed every other time you water.

Grey and Fuzzy Mould

Botrytis is a fungal disease that thrives in the presence of high humidity, attacking mostly young tender plants, which is why a terrarium is the perfect place for it to grow. Botrytis begins with tiny brown lesions before the plant is consumed by lots of grey spores. Affected leaves die and drop off the plant.

Rescue suggestion

Always monitor your terrarium, and at the first signs of botrytis forming, remove the infected leaf or leaves. If it's allowed to spread, the plant will likely die and the spores may infect neighbouring plants. Snip off leaves that are affected by mould and spray the contents of the terrarium with a chamomile water solution (page 96). Leave the lid open for 24–48 hours to allow air circulation.

Black/Brown Areas on Succulents and Cacti

Desert cacti, the majority of succulents and certain euphorbia (such as the cowboy cactus), require the brightest position in our homes to remain healthy.

There is little point investing in a desert cactus if you are unable to provide it with bright light. If it's positioned far away from a window it will likely die a long, slow death; you'd be better off buying a poster of a cactus.

In winter, when there isn't enough light or warmth for active growth, adding water to a potted cactus can have catastrophic results. Pathogens and bacteria thrive in moist soil, and together with a lack of oxygen, work to rot the roots. The first sign of this could be black or brown areas on the plant, which can be soft or firm.

Too much water/ lack of light

Brown or black areas can be a sign that the plant's roots are rotting. The decay can often start at the base of the stem, as this is the closest area to the soil and roots. There is very little you can do to save a cactus or succulent that is rotting from the base, other than chop off the healthy areas above the rotten area and propagate it (see page 233). If you do nothing, eventually the rot will kill the entire plant, so it's best to save what you can.

Root rot can also cause the top parts of the plant to shrivel or blacken. Check the health of the roots first: they should be firm, not mushy. If some roots are rotting and some still feel firm, follow the rescue suggestion in Yellow Leaves under 'too much water/lack of light' (see page 170). If the roots are firm, but the soil appears to be dry, and you haven't watered the cactus or succulent in the past month, pathogens may have entered the main plant itself (perhaps through a small wound) and are causing decay.

Rescue suggestion
For succulents, you can chop off the healthy part and propagate it (see page 233). For a cactus, try the steps below. This suggestion will leave permanent scars on the cactus, but better the plant is scarred than dead.
—   Sterilise a sharp knife and cut off the areas of decay, removing all signs of rot – even a tiny bit can spread.
—   Leave the cut areas to callous over and monitor the plant for further signs of decay.

Pest damage

See page 216.

Shrivelled and Wilted Succulent

Succulents grow in environments that other vegetation would not find favourable: they can be found in dry deserts, on high mountains and in cold regions where they have adapted to gather and store water in their leaves and stems. Some have further amazing adaptations that make efficient use of the limited amount of water available in their natural habitat. Crassulacean acid metabolism (or CAM) is one such adaptation (see page 42).

Normal leaf loss

Before you worry too much about the shrivelled, wilted leaves on your succulent, remember that old leaves are naturally discarded by the plant when they are no longer needed.

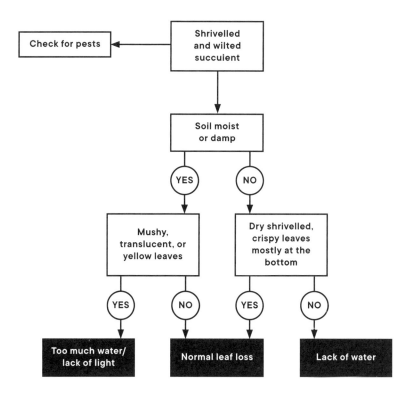

The old leaves at the base may be wilted and crispy, but this is perfectly normal and they can be picked off. If the leaves further up the plant are wilting, deflated, changing colour or they feel mushy, then this is likely a water/light issue.

Too much water/ lack of light

Succulents that aren't in bright light and are being watered frequently are at extreme risk of root rot. If they aren't in bright light, they aren't using water quickly and so it remains in the pot, causing the oxygen to deplete and bacteria to attack the roots. Poor soil, which is dense rather than light and airy, can contribute to the issue. A rotting succulent may have spongy, yellow, mushy, translucent leaves and/or black or brown areas of decay. The stem may turn brown/black, which can spread outwards to the leaves.

Rescue suggestion
Take the plant out of the pot to assess the roots. If they are mushy, the only way to salvage the plant is by propagating

a healthy leaf or by cutting the stem and propagating the top part, providing it is healthy (see page 233).

Despite being able to survive periods of drought, succulents need frequent watering during the warmer spring and summer months. The key to successful watering is in the soil – it needs to be very porous so that water can flow through it and out through the drainage holes. You can buy cacti and succulent potting mix or you can make your own (see page 80). Experiment by adding different media such as sand, grit and perlite.

Lack of water

The major difference between an underwatered and overwatered succulent is that the leaves of an underwatered plant won't be yellow or mushy; they're more likely to be shrivelled or brown and crispy. When water is depleted from the cells and not replaced, the cells will begin to collapse, giving the succulent leaves a wrinkled appearance.

Rescue suggestion

Check to see if the soil has become so compacted or dry that it is pulling away from the sides of the pot. If it has, aerate the soil by creating channels with a chopstick, and then hydrate the plant immediately. The best way to water it is from the bottom: sit the pot in a shallow dish of water and leave it there for 20–30 minutes to ensure the soil is completely saturated. Allow the water to drain from the pot before moving it back to its original spot.

Saving a dehydrated succulent may not be possible if the roots have died. If the plant hasn't recovered in 24–48 hours, despite being watered, it's unlikely to perk up. If there are any healthy parts of the plant remaining they can be propagated (see page 233).

Pest damage

See page 216.

Cacti Corking

Corking is a natural occurrence and although the appearance may suggest there is something wrong, it's just a normal part of the aging process. Corking (or lignification) is a browning and hardening of the stem, which usually begins at the base, but can also appear where there is branching. It has been suggested that corking is a way in which a plant ensures it is able to support further growth, which it does by hardening the stem. Corking is permanent, but doesn't harm your plant. There is nothing you can do about it so you may as well embrace your cactus's new and unique appearance.

Pests and Remedies

As much as we'd prefer insects not to attack our plants, an infestation isn't necessarily something to stress about. If you grow houseplants, it's likely that at some point you will encounter pests. Plants and pests go hand-in-hand – it's nature. Accept that your plants probably won't be pest-free forever, make peace with that, and when you spot signs of an infestation, remind yourself that insects are an important part of the ecosystem... then arm yourself with some horticultural soap and biological control.

There are literally hundreds of ideas on how to get rid of certain pests, some will work for some people but not for others. As with everything in plant care it's about experimenting and seeing what works for you. It's for that reason that I cannot give one solution that will absolutely rid your plants of a particular pest, but I can offer popular suggestions and include tips that have worked for me. Just because it isn't mentioned here, doesn't mean it won't work.

I have chosen to suggest methods that are environmentally friendly, harmless to the plant and, most importantly, effective in keeping pests under control. Most pests can be controlled by releasing predators that feed on them (biological control). The idea of this tends to freak some people out, but we already live with hundreds of insects in our homes, so really this shouldn't be an issue.

Treating pests is never simple, it takes time. Don't expect one treatment to eradicate the entire problem. The suggestions have to be repeated regularly to be effective.

The following pages will introduce you to the most common pests that impact houseplants – I haven't included whitefly, aphids or vine weevil as these are more commonly found on outdoor plants or plants that have been put outside over summer (that said, aphids can be easily removed by spraying the affected area with horticultural soap).

In terms of saving an infested plant, propagating a plant that has been infested by pests isn't something I recommend. Thrips lay their eggs in the tissue of all parts of the plant so it's likely they will emerge from propagated pieces, too. Juvenile scale is tricky to spot and mealybugs are very hard to eradicate, so it's not worth risking propagation for fear that the infestation will come back.

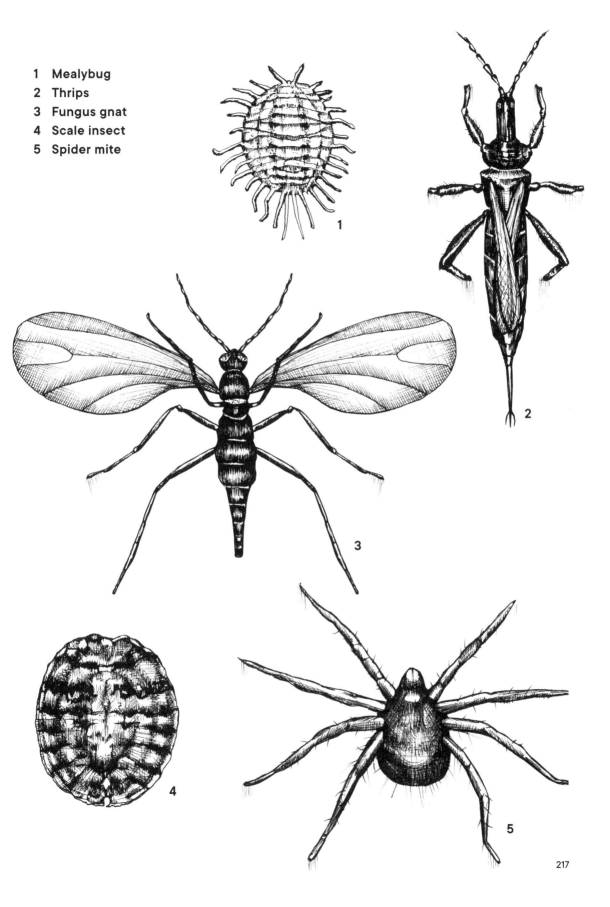

1 Mealybug
2 Thrips
3 Fungus gnat
4 Scale insect
5 Spider mite

Evilness rating

The pests mentioned have been rated on an 'evilness' scale from 1 to 5, with 5 being pure evil. This is an indication of how hard they are to control and how much damage they can cause to your plants.

Prevention is better than cure

— Don't bring pests into your house on a plant. Always make a very thorough examination of the plant before buying it. The same applies for plants that you buy online – examine them for signs of pests before nestling them into your collection.
— Make sure to give your plants enough light to grow. If they don't have enough light, they won't be using up water quickly, and soil that remains moist is an ideal breeding ground for bacteria and pests such as fungus gnats.
— Check your plants all the time. Get to know your plant and how it looks so you can identify any changes quickly. It is far easier to deal with a few pests than it is to tackle a full-on infestation.

Fungus gnats
Sciaridae

 1–2

Signs that your plant has fungus gnats

You'll see tiny black flies hanging out on the surface of the soil. They can also be seen flying haphazardly around the room. The greyish-brown flies are about 3mm in size with long legs that resemble those of a mosquito. The larvae look like tiny white maggots. Fungus gnats are usually seen on the surface of the soil but they can also enter the soil from the bottom of the pot through the drainage hole.

What are they?

These are small flies that feed on organic matter in the soil. They have four stages of development: eggs, larvae, pupae and adults. Eggs hatch in the soil about three days after laying, larvae take about 10 days to develop into pupae, then four days to develop into adults. Adults live for just over a week.

The adults don't damage the plant, but the larvae could potentially feed on roots, although they prefer decaying matter in the soil. An internet search will yield warnings that these gnats can kill your plant, and while it's true that the larvae can feed on the roots of seedlings and can cause them to die, gnats are unlikely to cause damage to an average-sized houseplant.

How much water you are giving your plant, in relation to the light it's receiving, is the biggest threat to your plant's health. Fungus gnats are more of a nuisance than a threat to the plant, but that's not to say you should just ignore them. They have been attracted to the soil because it's moist – and it is not good for the plant to sit in moist soil for a prolonged period of time. The appearance of these gnats is a warning that you need to adjust the amount of light and water your plant is getting.

Anyone who says fungus gnats killed their houseplant has probably overlooked the main cause for the plant dying, which is very likely to have been too much water and not enough light, leading to root rot.

Suggestions for control

Prevention is better than a cure – fungus gnats love moist soil, and the longer it remains moist the more appealing it is. Giving your plants enough light is the single best thing you can do to prevent fungus gnats.

To deal with the adults, use sticky fly traps – these are often yellow sticky cards that can be placed in and around the soil to catch the gnats.

Carnivorous plants such as cape sundews are great at attracting and capturing gnats on their leaves (see page 152). It's a good excuse to buy more plants! Dot them around the room near infested plants and see how many they catch.

To deal with the eggs and larvae, you have a couple of options to consider.

Option 1 Allow the soil to completely dry out, as this will make the soil an unappealing breeding ground and kill off some of the eggs and larvae while rendering others dormant. Doing this gives you a chance to capture as many of the adults as possible (with sticky traps or sundews) over the next few days without more hatching.

Option 2 Try biological control in the shape of beneficial nematodes, which are available to buy online. *Steinernema feltiae* are microscopic parasitic worms and when released into the soil they seek out the larvae, enter their bodies and digest them from the inside. This option is not cheap, but it works. Always follow the instructions on the product packet.

Scale insects
Coccoidea

 3–4

Signs that your plant has scale
Scale insects can range in size from around 1–10mm. Mature scale look like tiny round or oval brown scabs. Younger nymphs may have an orange/yellow appearance. They are usually found on the leaf veins, leaf joints and the stem. Sticky residue appears on the leaves, which the scale insects have excreted. A plant with an infestation may look limp or wilted (like a thirsty plant), leaves may turn yellow and fall off or show stunted growth. A black sooty mould may also be present where there are sticky pools of residue.

What are they?
Scale are sap-sucking insects that feed on plant phloem. They excrete unwanted sugars called honeydew or sap, leaving a sticky residue that appears on the leaves of infected plants. This sap can encourage the growth of sooty mould on the leaves. Newly hatched nymphs will crawl around the plant until they find a suitable spot to extract the sap, then they will become stationary and stay in that spot. They insert their mouthparts into the plant and feed on the sap. Once feeding has begun, they coat themselves with a tough waxy secretion that acts like a shell. Often you will see the insects in a line on the underside of a leaf along the vein.

Suggestions for control
To deal with the scale, you have several options:

Option 1 Cover the soil with a plastic bag so the scale insects don't fall on to the soil. Press strips of masking tape in areas where you see scale, then peel it off. The sticky tape removes the scale. Repeat this process on all areas of the plant. Discard the used tape. Spray the plant with horticultural soap, as this suffocates the insects. Repeat the process every 2–3 days.

Option 2 Firstly, follow option 1 above. Then use a biological control called scale control nematodes. Unlike regular nematodes, this is a solution that is sprayed on to the leaves of affected plants. The nematodes 'swim' on the film of water allowing them to enter the scale insects and kill them.

Option 3 When all else has failed and for serious infestations, take drastic action. I battled scale on a large umbrella tree for six months. It was badly infested and the leaves were too small and too many to make the masking tape approach effective. It's possible that the scale had been living on the tree for a year or more before I took it in and had been doing some serious damage. It was so beautiful, I didn't want to give up on it, but it was declining in health, losing leaves and overall vigour.

I cut each branch, about 30cm (1ft) below the leaves. I was left with only the woody stems of the tree and no leaves at all. I wasn't sure if it would work to eradicate all the scale, but thankfully it did. New leaves began to grow back with no signs of scale at all.

It's worth taking drastic action, if all else has failed, as it can save your plant from a slow death. This sort of action is best done in summer when there is enough warmth and bright light to help the plant regrow. Dramatically reduce the amount of water you give a plant that has no leaves, and place it outdoors or in an area that receives bright light to encourage new growth.

Spider mites
Tetranychidae

 3–4

Signs that your plant has spider mites
Spider mites are microscopic, so you have to look for evidence of their presence rather than the mites themselves. Fine webbing across the soil or under leaves is one such clue. Leaves can have white dust-like particles covering them and may look yellow, brown or wilted (or a combination of all three). Look out for fine stippling or mottling on the leaves where the cells have died. To confirm an infestation, hold a piece of light-coloured paper under the plant leaves and shake the plant gently: tiny red, white, yellow, black or brown specks that fall on to the paper are mites. Spider mites can infest your plants at any time of the year but they love warm dry air so are particularly prevalent in winter and spring when central heating tends to make our homes warm and dry.

What are they?
Spider mites don't live in the soil, they live on the plant, creating webs in which to attach their eggs. Eggs can hatch in as little as three days and up to 20 days depending on the conditions. As soon as the larvae emerge, they begin feeding

on the sap from plant cells using needle-like mouthparts to puncture the leaf. A female adult typically lives for 2–4 weeks and is capable of laying several hundred eggs. They are easily missed because, unlike other plant pests, they are barely the size of a pinhead. As soon as they have colonised a plant, they start looking for others.

Suggestions for control

Option 1 The easiest, but not necessarily most effective, option is to take the plant to the shower and spray it. If it doesn't need watering, cover the soil with a plastic bag so it doesn't get wet. Make sure to spray the undersides of the leaves. Wipe the plant with a cloth. Repeat every three days.

Option 2 Spray the whole plant with horticultural soap, paying particular attention to the base and undersides of the leaves where webs are present. The soap only kills the adults, so spraying has to be repeated every three days to kill the emerging larvae.

Option 3 Use a biological control called *Phytoseiulus persimilis* (PP), which are mites that feed on the eggs, larvae and adults. Spider mites prefer a warm, dry environment, whereas PPs prefer humidity, so run a humidifier near the plant if you can. PPs are hard to see because they are very small, so don't be concerned if you can't see them after releasing them. If you have spider mites on indoor citrus plants you need to use *Amblyseius andersoni* mites as PPs aren't as effective at killing citrus spider mites.

Option 4 If spider mites have damaged most of the leaves on a plant, you may decide to chop it back and allow it to regrow. This is best done in summer. Cut all the damaged leaves off (that may be all of them), spray with horticultural soap and put the plant in a bright, warm position near a window to encourage regrowth. Monitor for signs of reinfestation (spraying with soap if necessary). Reduce watering as there are fewer or no leaves.

Spider mites prefer warm, dry, environments. After treatment, run a humidifier as a deterrent.

Mealybugs
Pseudococcidae

 4–5

Signs that your plant has mealybugs

A juvenile mealybug can be white, tinged with pink, orange or yellow and is approximately 1–2mm in size. The adults resemble a tiny, white, woolly woodlouse, and are approximately 3–5mm in size. The first sign of their arrival is white waxy or fluffy areas in the leaf joints (where the petiole joins the stem). The bugs are often well hidden, choosing areas under leaves and in crevices, which can be especially hard to see on compact succulents. A plant with an infestation may have yellow leaves (with or without brown margins), wilted brown leaves, loss of overall vigour, stunted growth and even leaf loss. There may also be honeydew on the leaves causing black sooty mould.

What are they?

The main mealybug species that infest houseplants in the UK are the glasshouse, long-tailed and citrus mealybug. Glasshouse mealybugs are the ones most commonly found on houseplants, including cacti and succulents. Mealybugs are prolific breeders, laying up to 600 eggs in a period of 5–10 days, which, if there are more than 8–10 insects on the plant, makes successful eradication extremely difficult. It only takes one mealybug on one plant to infest many plants in your collection. They don't tend to move far, but will crawl to neighbouring plants if they are close by.

Mealybugs suck the phloem from plants using mouthparts that pierce the plant cells. They excrete excess sugars in the form of honeydew, which can attract mould to grow on the leaves. Certain species, such as citrus mealybugs, inject toxic saliva into the plant as they feed, causing additional problems, such as leaf deformity. Adult males are tiny and have wings, and they live for only a few days (you will probably never see these); females are wingless, but crawl. Males die after mating, the females mature, lay eggs, and die soon after. The complete life-cycle takes 25–50 days.

Suggestions for control

Option 1 Individual mealybugs can be killed by directly applying surgical spirit onto them. This is only effective if you have a very small infestation (1–4 bugs) and you can be sure that you have treated every single mealybug. Any more than five mealybugs and you have a war on your hands.

Option 2 This option is only for cacti. Mealybugs favour warmer temperatures (18–24°C is optimum for reproduction), so taking your plant outside in colder weather can slow down this rate and even kill them. Most cacti can tolerate temperatures just a few degrees above freezing, so if you have an infestation, put the plant outside in winter for two or three days and this will potentially kill the mealybugs. Remove them by spraying the plant with water or picking them off with tweezers. Spray with horticultural soap.

Option 3 The most efficient predator of mealybugs is *Cryptolaemus montrouzieri* – the brown Australian ladybird. The ladybirds can be ordered as larvae or adults. Before releasing them, you must place the plant in a room or in a container that can be sealed, or cover the plant in a large plastic bag with very small air holes pierced through the bag, as this ensures neither the larvae or ladybirds escape. To do their job, they need several hours of bright sunlight and temperatures of at least 20°C.

Root mealybugs
Rhizoecus species

 4–5

Signs that your plant has root mealybugs
If you have a plant that isn't growing despite being in good light, is showing symptoms of a decline in health, has pale leaves or starts losing leaves, or has mealybugs on its leaves, root mealybugs may be the cause. If this is the case, it's time to check the roots. Tip the plant out of its pot and look for a white fungus-like substance on the roots or on the inside of the pot. Closer inspection with a magnifying glass may reveal tiny white insects (around 1–1.5mm) feeding on the roots, although these are hard to spot, particularly if the soil contains perlite. The presence of a white powdery substance around the inside of the pot and on the roots is the most obvious sign that root mealybugs are in the soil.

What are they?
Just when you thought mealybugs couldn't get any worse, these guys come along. The *Rhizoecus* species of mealybug live in the soil and feed on the roots in much the same way as other species feed on the plant above the soil line, piercing the root and sucking on the sap.

Suggestions for control

Option 1 Take the plant out of the pot, remove all of the soil, cut off damaged or infected roots. Then rinse the roots with water in a diluted solution of horticultural soap. You can also fill a small container with the diluted soap and soak the roots for 10-15 minutes. Remove the plant and rinse the roots under running water. Repot the plant in a new pot (or wash the old one with boiling water and soap) and use fresh soil. Water.

Option 2 Soak the roots in hot water. This is an option worth trying, but it's difficult to get right as the temperature has to be maintained for 10 minutes. It should also only be tried as a last resort as the heat may damage the roots. To give it a go, remove the plant from the pot, gently knock off the lower third of the soil, and cut away any damaged or infected roots. Heat a pan of water to 48°C (the ideal temperature for killing mealybugs, eggs and larvae). Soak the roots in the pan for 10 minutes, maintaining the temperature. Repot the plant in a new pot (or wash the old one with boiling water and soap) and use fresh soil. Water.

Option 3 Use a biological control called *Stratiolaelaps scimitus*, which is known to feed on fungus gnat larvae, thrips pupae, root aphids and root mealybugs. They may also move up the plant foliage and feed on mealybugs above the soil.

Option 4 You may take the decision to sacrifice this plant to protect the others in your collection. I'm ok with that.

Thrips
Thysanoptera
 5

Signs that your plant has thrips
The only good thing about thrips is the damage is very visible and very specific to thrips, so identification is straightforward. Signs include scars or silvery sunken patches on leaves or stems that turn brown. You might also see tiny black dots of excrement around the patches. New leaves are often stunted, papery and deformed. The majority of leaves will be damaged unless the thrips are detected early.

What are they?
Dark, thin-bodied insects around 1–2mm in length. They have narrow wings, but it's unlikely you'll see them flying around.

If you see small insects flying near your plants, they will probably be fungus gnats (see page 218) rather than thrips, which tend to hop from plant to plant. They lay eggs on or into plant tissue, the larvae hatch and puncture the plant cells with their mouthparts to suck out the sap. They are particularly fond of young leaves; sometimes a leaf will unfurl that has already been damaged by feeding thrips. Why do they have the highest evil rating of all pests? Because once they are in your house, they can infest most of your plants, making it a very difficult task to eradicate them.

Suggestions for control

Option 1 Use masking tape to remove the thrips you can see. Press strips of tape onto the leaves and pull away – this will remove the adults, larvae and eggs, which are very difficult to see. Once you've done this, spray the plant with horticultural soap – it's best to cover the soil with a plastic bag when spraying the plant to prevent any thrips being dislodged and falling into the soil. This whole process must be repeated every 3–4 days.

    The problem with sprays is that thrips are well hidden on the plant, so the chances of getting rid of them with any type of spray aren't that favourable. If you do go for option 1, be prepared for it to be an ongoing treatment.

Option 2 Spray the plant with horticultural soap, then leave it to dry. Use a biological control of predatory mites – there are several options to choose from. *Stratiolaelaps scimitus* feed on fungus gnat larvae, root mealybugs and thrip larvae, but they don't eat the adults – so these can be good for keeping down the infestation. *Amblyseius andersoni* mites also feed on the larvae. *Orius laevigatus* will feed on all stages of a thrip (egg, larvae and adult) and this is The Terminator of biological control – hasta la vista thrips.

Fungus gnat caught on a cape sundew

Scale on a stem

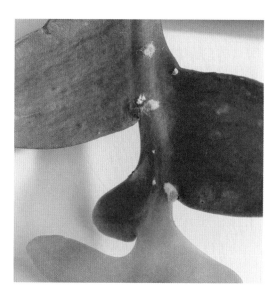

Mealybugs on a leaf

Propagation

If you have only one plant, there will (with a few exceptions) be a way of propagating it to make another. Propagating can also be a way to 'save' a dying plant; the plant itself may not survive, but by propagating it, a part of it lives on.

There are many ways of propagating a plant, and different methods will suit different plants, which is why knowing the species is important. As a general guide (but of course, there are exceptions) a plant that has firm and fleshy leaves (such as succulent leaves) will root from the leaf itself, whereas plants with thin or large leaves usually root from a stem cutting.

When we propagate a plant by taking a cutting, we're advised to take the cutting from specific areas of the plant, which differ depending on the species. This relates to the totipotency of the cells in that particular area of the plant. Some plants have totipotent power (which means they can regenerate from cells), but not all cells have the totipotency to develop into a new plant. This can be demonstrated by the fiddle leaf fig – if you remove a leaf and put it in water it will grow roots, but it's very unlikely to develop into a plant. Cells in the stem, however, do have the potential to grow into a new plant, which is why you should propagate a fiddle leaf fig stem cutting or use the air layer method, rather than just stick a leaf in water.

Sometimes the stem and the leaves of the same plant can be propagated, so it's worth trying both to see which works – it can be an interesting experiment to see which grows roots first. Often roots will begin to show within 2–6 weeks, depending on the plant, light and warmth, but don't be disheartened if a cutting or leaf fails. Propagating is a lottery, and some attempts will work while others won't – don't let that put you off having another go or trying another method.

Stem Cutting

Taking cuttings is one of the easiest and cheapest ways to increase your plant collection. Stems that will root tend to have nodes – this is the bumpy point where a leaf joins the stem – and it's from these nodes that roots form when the stem is propagated in soil or water.

Stem cutting in water or soil

One of the most popular methods is cutting a stem or leaf and putting it in water. While this works well, you might also consider propagating in soil.
—   Fill a clean jar with water or fill a pot with a chunky, free-draining potting mix (such as houseplant soil with added bark, coir and perlite).
—   With clean scissors or a sharp knife, cut a stem just below a node.
—   Insert the cutting into the jar or pot (remove any leaves that may end up being submerged in water).
—   Place the jar or pot in moderate to bright indirect light.
—   For stem cuttings in water, change the water once a week and every time the water becomes discoloured to ensure a regular supply of oxygen is present.

Transferring the cutting to soil

Transferring water-propagated plants into soil is best attempted when the roots are about 2.5–5cm (1–2in) long.
—   Fill the bottom of a small pot with about 5cm (2in) of free-draining potting mix.
—   Take the rooted cutting out of the jar or glass and rinse the roots with fresh water. Place the cutting in and fill around the roots with soil, leaving space at the top of the pot for watering.
—   Pour water through the soil until it flows out of the bottom of the pot. The soil needs to be fully saturated as the roots are used to being very wet.
—   Water again when the soil is approaching dry.

Propagating Succulents and Cacti

There are many ways to successfully propagate succulents and cacti, and it's worth experimenting to see what works best for you and your plants.

Succulent division

If you have a clump-forming succulent such as an aloe, haworthia or agave, you can propagate by division (see page 239).

Self-propagating succulents

Some succulents don't need human intervention and will simply drop a leaf onto the soil below and form roots, and as if by magic, a tiny plantlet will appear. If you'd like to try this manually, simply snap or twist off a whole leaf (from the point where it meets the stem) and place it on top of a free-draining potting mix. When roots begin to form, use a misting spray to occasionally moisten the soil. Once the plantlet has fully formed, the original leaf will decompose or you can remove it.

Succulent stem cutting

Another option is to cut the stem of a succulent and place it in a pot of soil.
— Use a pair of clean, sharp scissors to cut through a piece of stem.
— You can set this aside for a few days to let the end heal, but this isn't absolutely necessary – I've had success without doing this.
— Push the cut end into fresh, dry potting mix. I suggest dry soil to avoid the end rotting.
— After a few days, lightly water or mist the soil.

Kalanchoe

Kalanchoe babies can be carefully removed from the leaf blade with your fingers and simply placed into potting mix. Moisten with a spray bottle. Leave to develop roots, then use a small spoon to separate the rooted plantlets into pots.

Cacti stem cutting

Cacti can be propagated by cutting the stem.
— Using gloves or tongs to hold the cactus, make a clean cut through the stem with a sharp knife.
— Leave the cutting to dry for 2–3 days before planting. This is necessary to allow the cut to heal and protect it from rotting.

- Plant the cutting into dry cacti and succulent soil, packing the soil in around the stem to hold it in position.
- After a few days, lightly water or mist the soil.
- Be patient, it can take weeks or months for roots to grow.

Cacti offsets, pads and pups

Most cacti produce 'pads', 'joints' or 'offsets' that can be detached or cut off and propagated into new plants. These might form at the base of the plant, but some also form along the stem or even on the pads (these are paddle-shaped growths on plants such as opuntia). In the wild, an offset (new segment), sometimes called a 'pup' can naturally drop off and self-propagate.
- Wear gloves. Use your fingers to twist the offset to remove it from the parent plant. You can also use a clean, sharp knife to remove it if manual twisting isn't working.
- You may choose to let the end callous over for a few days, but success is possible without doing this.
- Press the offset gently into dry cacti and succulent potting mix.
- After a few days, lightly water or mist the soil.

Whole Leaf

Begonias, peperomias, hoyas and African violets will all root from a whole leaf cutting.
- Use a clean, sharp knife to remove a leaf together with the short stem attaching it to the plant (the petiole).
- Trim the petiole so it's about 3–4cm (1–1.5in) long.
- Fill a glass bottle (or a similar vessel that has a narrow opening at the top) with water and place the leaf into the water so that the bottom part of the petiole is submerged. Alternatively, fill a pot with a free-draining potting mix.
- Place on a bright windowsill.
- For a cutting in water, keep an eye on the water level and ensure it doesn't dip below the bottom of the stem. When roots develop, pot up into fresh, free-draining potting mix.
- For a cutting in a pot, water when the soil is almost dry.

ZZ plant

It also couldn't be simpler to propagate the ZZ plant (*Zamioculcas zamiifolia*) from a leaf, both in potting mix and in water, although it can take many months for the rhizomes to develop.

You can use the Leaf Section technique outlined below, or insert a leaf straight into a free-draining potting mix. Place the potted leaf in bright light and don't allow the soil to completely dry out. This is a slow process that requires patience, but it's fascinating to see the rhizomes develop.

Leaf Section

Begonia

Another interesting propagation technique to try with begonias is cutting a leaf into triangles or sections.
—   Select a young healthy leaf from a plant that has been recently watered (the plant must be turgid or the leaf may shrivel).
—   Use a clean, sharp knife to remove the leaf and leaf stem (petiole) from the base of the plant.
—   Cut the leaf into triangles, from the outside to the centre of the leaf.
—   Put each section, pointed-end down, into a free-draining potting mix. Press the soil around them so they are firmly in place, standing upright.
—   Water lightly, just to settle the soil.
—   Cover with a cloche, or secure a clear plastic bag (pierced with small holes) over the pot using an elastic band. Open the cloche or bag once a week to allow for air circulation.
—   Place in warm spot with moderate to bright light.

Instead of cutting the begonia leaf into sections you can instead make small incisions.
—   Make incisions along the veins underneath the leaf about 2.5cm (1in) apart. Don't cut all the way through the leaf, only score the vein.
—   Lightly moisten a tray or pot filled with potting mix. Place the whole leaf, vein side down, into the soil. Place a few small pebbles on top of the leaf so the veins remain in contact with the soil.
—   Cover with a cloche or a clear plastic bag punctured with

small holes and secured with an elastic band. Position in a warm bright spot.
— Open the cloche or bag once a week to allow for air circulation. Young plants will form where the cuts were made in the veins.
— Once baby plantlets have formed, gently cut or tear away the leaf of the parent plant from around the plantlets and scoop each baby out with a spoon. These can then be potted up.

Snake plant

Leaf section propagation can also be done with a snake plant.
— Remove a healthy leaf from the base of the plant.
— Using a clean, sharp knife cut the leaf into sections that are about 7.5cm (3in) wide.
— Insert each cutting, cut end down, into a moist potting mix. Firm the soil around the cuttings.
— Place in a warm, bright position. Water again when the soil is completely dry.
— Be patient, it takes time for the roots of baby plantlets to form.

Runners and Offsets

Propagating runners

Some plants grow runners, including the spider plant and strawberry begonia. These specialised stems (called stolons) emerge from the parent plant and produce babies. It's possible to propagate the babies while they are still attached to the parent plant.
— Fill a small pot (or several pots if you have a few runners) with lightly moistened potting mix and place it near the parent plant so the baby plant can reach it.
— Secure the base of the baby plant into the small pot ensuring it remains attached to the parent plant. Use an unfurled paper clip to help secure it into the soil.
— Add water only when the soil is approaching dry.
— Once the baby plant begins to grow roots and new leaves, cut the stolon, which joins it to the parent plant.

Propagating offsets

Many tropical houseplants produce baby versions of themselves that can easily be separated from the parent plant to create a new plant – the Chinese money plant (*Pilea peperomioides*) is one example. The plantlets emerge from the stem, either under the soil or above.

- Wait until the offset is about 5–10cm (2–4in) tall. The longer you leave it to grow attached to the parent plant, the better its chance of survival.
- Remove the whole plant from the grow pot and move the soil with your fingers so you can locate where the baby is growing from. Cut it off the parent plant with a clean, sharp knife. Place the offset in a glass of water, so the base of the stem is submerged.
- Once a healthy root system has formed, the plant can be potted up into free-draining potting mix.
- If you find a plantlet that already has its own roots, just cut it off the parent and plant straight into free-draining soil. Water lightly and place in moderate to bright light.

Ponytail palm

The ponytail palm (*Beaucarnea recurvata*) also produces offsets near the base of its bulbous trunk. Wait until the offset is around 10–20cm (4–8in) tall, then remove the parent plant from its pot and very carefully cut off the baby plant using a clean, sharp knife. The offset may or may not have roots. Plant the offset directly into a lightly moistened potting mix suitable for cacti and succulents. Depending on light and warmth, roots should form in 1–2 months.

Bromeliads

Certain plants, such as bromeliads will only bloom once but will grow offsets, which can be removed, propagated and will bloom when they reach maturity.

- Using a clean, sharp knife cut the offset from the base of the parent plant.
- Remove any papery, brown leaves from around the base of the plantlet.
- Fill a pot with cacti and succulent potting mix. Place the base of the plantlet into the soil and use a small cane to support it upright.
- Water and place in a warm, bright spot. Water again when the soil is completely dry.

Cane Cuttings

Use this technique to propagate plants such as yuccas and dracaenas that have lost all or most of their leaves. It's important that the yucca cane is firm to the press and not mushy or soft (and therefore rotten).

— Cut through the cane using a clean, sharp knife (leave the wax on the top section if it has any).
— Fill a small pot with lightly moistened, free-draining potting mix. Insert the cut section, bare end down, so that at least half of the stem is submerged. Firm the soil around the cane.
— Secure a cloche or a clear plastic bag punctured with small holes around the pot using an elastic band.
— Place in a bright warm spot. Open the cloche or bag once a week to allow for air circulation and to check the soil for moisture. Water when dry.
— Remove the bag when shoots appear.

Division

If you have a houseplant that's busting out of its pot, you might choose to divide it rather than move it into a bigger pot. Dividing a plant that has become congested is a great way to give it more room to grow without having to go up a pot size – you'll also gain extra plants to give away, swap or hoard.

Clump-forming plants

Clump-forming plants such as aspidistras, African violets, the peace lily, spider plant, prayer plant and many alocasias can be divided by teasing apart the clumps, each of which have their own root balls.
— Remove the plant from the pot. Use your fingers to remove some of the soil so you can see the roots.
— Gently tease apart the individual root balls (it may be necessary to cut some of the roots or rhizomes with a clean pair of scissors or a knife).
— Pot each clump into fresh potting mix. Water them and place them in moderate to bright indirect light.
— Don't be worried if they droop, they will be adjusting to life alone and should perk up within a week or so.

Non-clump-forming plants

It may sound drastic, but you can effectively cut a plant in half and gain two for the price of one. To determine if you can divide a plant into two, take it out of the pot and examine the roots. If they form a dense mass and there is enough top growth to sustain two plants, you may decide to go for the chop. Ferns, such as Boston and asparagus, can be divided by cutting the root ball into sections.

—   Remove the plant from the pot. Use a sharp clean knife to slice through the top of the soil, straight down through the root ball as if you're cutting a cake. You can cut the root ball into halves or quarters, depending on how many plants you'd like.
—   Pot each section into fresh potting mix. Water and leave the plants to settle.
—   Place in bright indirect light to recuperate.

Rhizomes and Tubers

Each piece of rhizome or tuber has the potential to develop into a new plant. They store energy in the form of starch, proteins and other nutrients that can be used to grow roots, from which a new plant can form. Popular plants such as caladiums, oxalis and alocasias produce tubers. Simply take the plant out of the pot and search the soil for fleshy pebble-like growths, remove as many as you like and pot them up in potting mix.

Rabbit's foot fern

One of my favourite plants to propagate by its rhizomes is the rabbit's foot fern. Its furry rhizomes appear like tarantula legs and they live on the surface of the soil.

—   Snip off a furry 'leg' and ensure it includes a section of foliage.
—   Fill a pot or tray with potting mix and lightly moisten it. Lie the cutting horizontally across the top of the soil.
—   Secure it in place with an unfurled paperclip.
—   Cover with a cloche or use a clear plastic bag punctured with small holes and secure around the pot with an elastic band. Place somewhere warm and bright.
—   Remove the cloche or bag once a week for air circulation and to check the soil for moisture. Water when dry.

Air Layering

Air layering is a good way to propagate woody or branching plants, or to reduce the size of a very tall plant. The parent plant remains intact until roots have formed where the incision is made, then it can be cut off and planted. You end up with a much larger plant than you would using other methods of propagation, but it does take much longer. Patience is a must with this technique.

— Fill a small, clear plastic bag with lightly moistened peat-free garden compost and secure at the top with an elastic band. Make sure the bag is full.

— Select the branch or section of trunk that you would like to make a new plant from. You need a clear 10cm (4in) section of stem to make the incisions – remove a few leaves if necessary.

— Using a clean, sharp knife make a cut approximately 2–3mm deep in the stem, just below a node. Cut all the way around the circumference of the stem but don't cut all the way through it.

— Make another cut approximately 4–5cm (1.5–2in) above the first one. Then peel back the woody top layer to expose the creamy-white tissue underneath.

— Lightly scrape the exposed area up and down with the edge of a knife.

— Brush with rooting hormone (this is optional).

— Lay the bag of soil on its side and slice it open lengthwise.

— Slot the cut area of the bag over the wounded area of the stem.

— Close the bag by overlapping the cut sides together around the stem and wrap string firmly around the bag to secure it.

— When you see lots of roots in the bag, you can cut all the way through the stem beneath the bag, near to where the new roots have formed.

— Your new plant is ready to pot up. It may need staking to keep it upright until the root system has fully developed.

Simple Layering

This works well with string of pearls – simply coil a strand so that the pearls are in contact with the top of the soil and secure in place with an unfurled paperclip. Simple layering is an easy way to propagate vining plants such as devil's ivy and heartleaf philodendron, using these instructions.

— Fill one (or a few) small pots with potting mix and moisten with water.
— Place the pots around the plant.
— Select a vine with an aerial root bud or node and secure the section and the root bud into the soil. Use an unfurled paperclip to hold the vine in place. The root bud should be in contact with the soil.
— Roots will form from the bud and then the vine can be cut from the parent plant.
— This can be done with as many pots as you like.

Pruning

As plants grow, their shape will change: lower leaves are discarded when they are no longer needed, stems lengthen, new leaves may be smaller or larger than the original ones, vining plants may become straggly. Loving how a plant grows and letting it just be isn't always the kindest attitude to take – a tidy up is not only good for its appearance, but also for the overall health of the plant. A prune can help to support new, healthy growth and a bushier and more vigorous plant.

You can opt for a light trim, removing some of the dead leaves and long straggly vines, or you can renovate and reinvigorate an entire plant by completely chopping it back to just above the soil. Light pruning and grooming can be done at any time of the year, but a dramatic chop should be done just before spring to ensure the plant can take advantage of the warmer and brighter days to recover.

Never prune a plant and move straight on to the next without cleaning your scissors or secateurs. You could spread pests or disease to other plants.

Trim

Here are some general trimming tips for a variety of different plants.

— Remove leaves and leaf sheaths that are brown, wilted and papery. Pick off dead, shrivelled leaves from the base of the plant.

— Remove dead flowers (they can encourage the growth of grey mould if left to decompose).

— Trim back any long vines that have few leaves, spaced far apart. This will encourage the plant to become fuller as well as looking less straggly.

— Cut off leaves or stems that are damaged or broken.

— Remove the tips of stems (above the last node) to encourage growth lower down, helping to create a bushier appearance.

Chop

Most tropical houseplants can be chopped to just above the soil and will regrow, apart from a few exceptions such as orchids and palms (do a bit of research on the particular plant before you do anything drastic).

If a plant has been through the wars with pests and most of the leaves are damaged, or if you are fighting a pest infestation but just can't seem to get on top of it, consider going for a chop. I have had great success with cutting back plants, but you must give them bright light to regrow. Watching it produce new leaves is like being given a second chance to care for it better.

Acknowledgements

I'm forever grateful to my husband James and daughter Eva for accepting cactus-related injuries as a normal part of life. Mum and Dad, I want to thank you for instilling in me a love of nature from an early age, and to my brother, thank you for trying to keep plants alive, I know it hasn't always worked out.

To all my friends, please know you are an integral part of me and this book. Every single one of you has contributed in some way to making this happen. Special thanks to Ruth Greatrex for providing the illustrations – who would have thought that meeting all those years ago at art college would lead to this!

Thank you to Clare Hulton for your guidance, and to the whole team at Bloomsbury for holding my hand through this process and making this book possible. A special thanks to Zena Alkayat for making this book the very best it could be. Hyperkit, Tim Balaam and Kate Sclater, thank you for designing something I am very proud to have my name on.

When my plants asked if they could be photographed by Emily Stein and assistant Ken Street, I thought they were crazy for even thinking such an amazing, talented pair would agree – but you were both game, and we are incredibly grateful. Emily, Ken and Ruth, this book is as much yours as it is mine.

Huge thank you to Emily and Mark at Happy Houseplants (happyhouseplants.co.uk), Pete and Niki (@the_jungle_rooms) and Leigh Message for opening your home to us.

Further thanks to: MAP Stores (mapstores.co.uk); RAFT St Albans (raftfurniture.co.uk); Anthropologie – thank you Alice Sykes! (anthropologie.com); Burston Garden Centre (burston.co.uk); and Anther & Moss (antherandmoss.com).

Index

BLOOMSBURY PUBLISHING
Bloomsbury Publishing Plc
50 Bedford Square, London, WC1B 3DP, UK
29 Earlsfort Terrace, Dublin 2, Ireland

BLOOMSBURY, BLOOMSBURY PUBLISHING and the Diana logo
are trademarks of Bloomsbury Publishing Plc

First published in Great Britain 2022

A catalogue record for this book is available from the British Library.

Library of Congress Cataloguing-in-Publication data has been applied for.

ISBN: HB: 978-1-5266-3813-7; eBook: 978-1-5266-3812-0

10 9 8 7 6 5 4 3 2 1

Project Editor: Zena Alkayat
Designer: Hyperkit
Photographer: Emily Stein
Prop Stylist: Sarah Gerrard-Jones
Illustrator: Ruth Greatrex
Proofreader: Helen Griffin
Indexer: Vanessa Bird

Printed and bound in China by C&C Offset Printing Ltd.

MIX
Paper from
responsible sources
FSC® C008047

To find out more about our authors and books visit www.bloomsbury.com
and sign up for our newsletters.